NOTORIOUS PIRATES GRAPHICS

BLACKBEARD
FEARED PIRATE CAPTAIN

text by Jessica Gunderson

illustrated by Andi Espinosa ✦ color by Jose Ramos

CAPSTONE PRESS
a capstone imprint

Published by Capstone Press, an imprint of Capstone
1710 Roe Crest Drive, North Mankato, Minnesota 56003
capstonepub.com

Copyright © 2025 by Capstone. All rights reserved. No part of this publication may be reproduced in whole or in part, or stored in a retrieval system, or transmitted in any form or by any means, electronic, mechanical, photocopying, recording, or otherwise, without written permission of the publisher.

Library of Congress Cataloging-in-Publication Data
Names: Gunderson, Jessica, author. | Espinosa, Andi, illustrator.
Title: Blackbeard, feared pirate captain / by Jessica Gunderson ; illustrated by Andi Espinosa.
Description: North Mankato, Minnesota : Capstone Press, [2025] | Series: Notorious pirates graphics | Includes bibliographical references. | Audience: Ages 9-11 | Audience: Grades 4-6 | Summary: "Little is known about Edward Teach's life before he became known as the fearsome pirate Blackbeard. But during the golden age of piracy, he ruled the seas along the coast of the North American colonies and beyond. Learn more about Blackbeard's adventures and how he became one of the most infamous—and feared—pirate captains of all time in a graphic novel filled with deception, plunder, and more."—Provided by publisher.
Identifiers: LCCN 2023046192 (print) | LCCN 2023046193 (ebook) | ISBN 9781669069652 (hardcover) | ISBN 9781669069607 (paperback) | ISBN 9781669069614 (pdf) | ISBN 9781669069621 (epub) | ISBN 9781669069638 (kindle edition)
Subjects: LCSH: Teach, Edward, -1718—Juvenile literature. | Teach, Edward, -1718—Comic books, scripts, etc. | Pirates—Biography—Juvenile literature. | Pirates—Biography—Comic books, scripts, etc. | CYAC: Graphic novels. | LCGFT: Biographical comics. | Graphic novels.
Classification: LCC G537.T4 G86 2025 (print) | LCC G537.T4 (ebook) | DDC 910.4/5—dc23/eng/20240214
LC record available at https://lccn.loc.gov/2023046192
LC ebook record available at https://lccn.loc.gov/2023046193

Editorial Credits
Editor: Alison Deering; Designer: Elijah Blue; Production Specialist: Tori Abraham

Any additional websites and resources referenced in this book are not maintained, authorized, or sponsored by Capstone. All product and company names are trademarks™ or registered® trademarks of their respective holders.

Printed and bound in the USA. 5853

CONTENTS

INTRODUCTION... 4

CHAPTER 1
QUEEN ANNE'S REVENGE........................... 6

CHAPTER 2
NO MERCY!.. 14

CHAPTER 3
PIRATE PROBLEM.. 20

CHAPTER 4
RAIDS AND RANSOM.. 26

CHAPTER 5
SAFE HARBORS.. 34

MORE ABOUT BLACKBEARD............... 44
GLOSSARY.. 46
OTHER BOOKS IN THIS SERIES.......... 47
INTERNET SITES... 47
ABOUT THE CREATORS........................ 48

INTRODUCTION

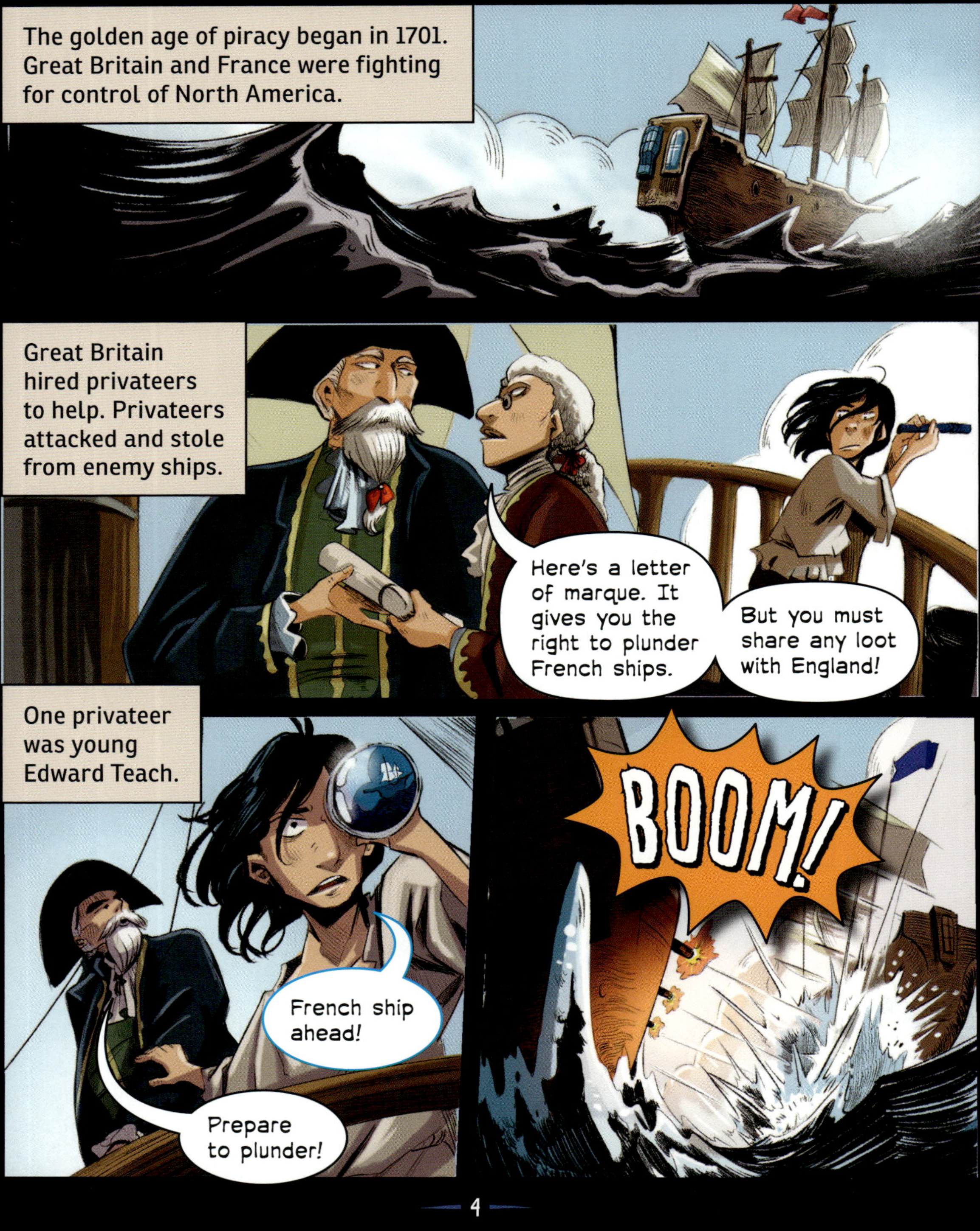

The golden age of piracy began in 1701. Great Britain and France were fighting for control of North America.
Great Britain hired privateers to help. Privateers attacked and stole from enemy ships.
Here's a letter of marque. It gives you the right to plunder French ships.
But you must share any loot with England!
One privateer was young Edward Teach.
French ship ahead!
Prepare to plunder!
BOOM!

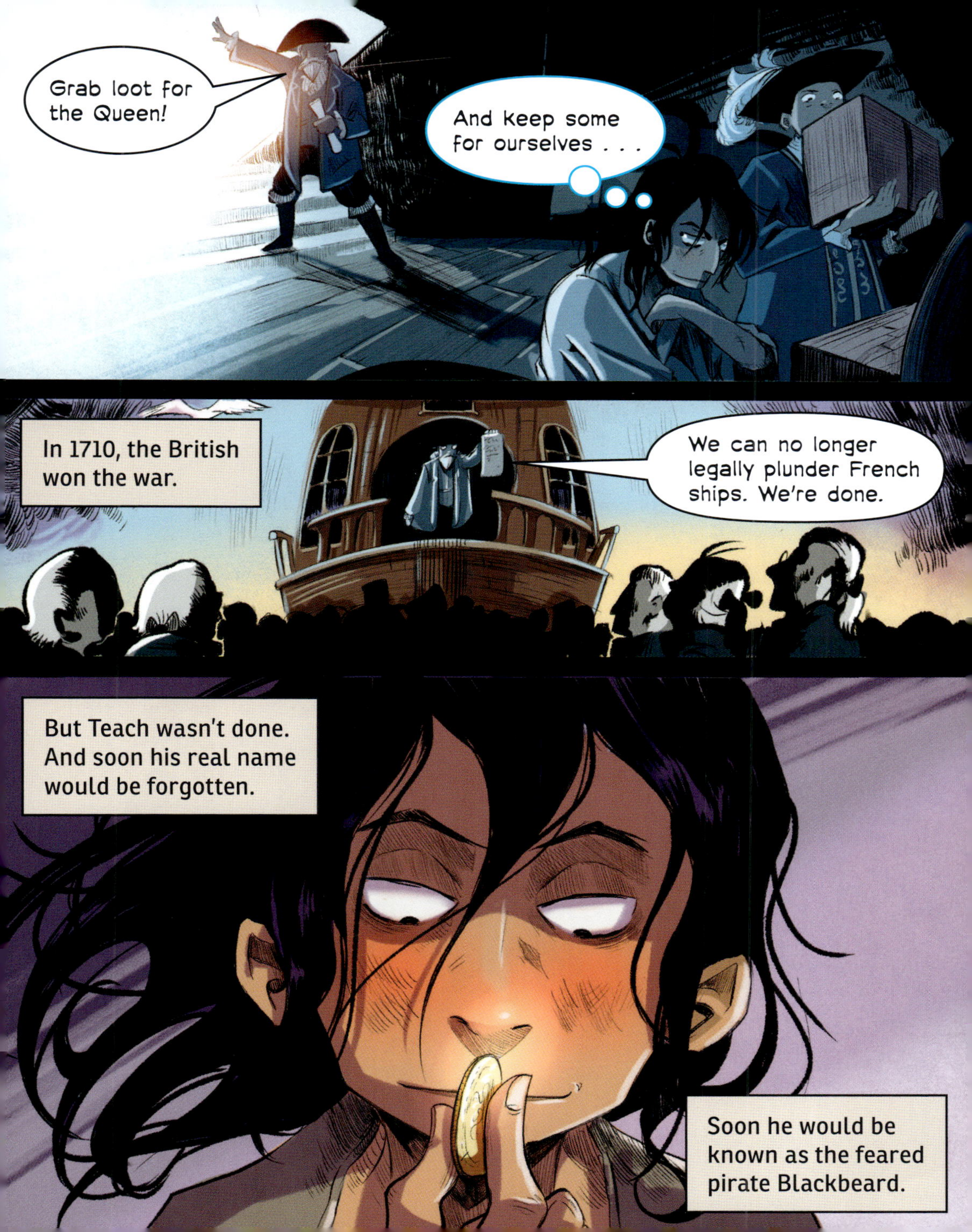
Grab loot for the Queen!
And keep some for ourselves . . .
In 1710, the British won the war.
We can no longer legally plunder French ships. We're done.
But Teach wasn't done. And soon his real name would be forgotten.
Soon he would be known as the feared pirate Blackbeard.

CHAPTER 1

QUEEN ANNE'S REVENGE

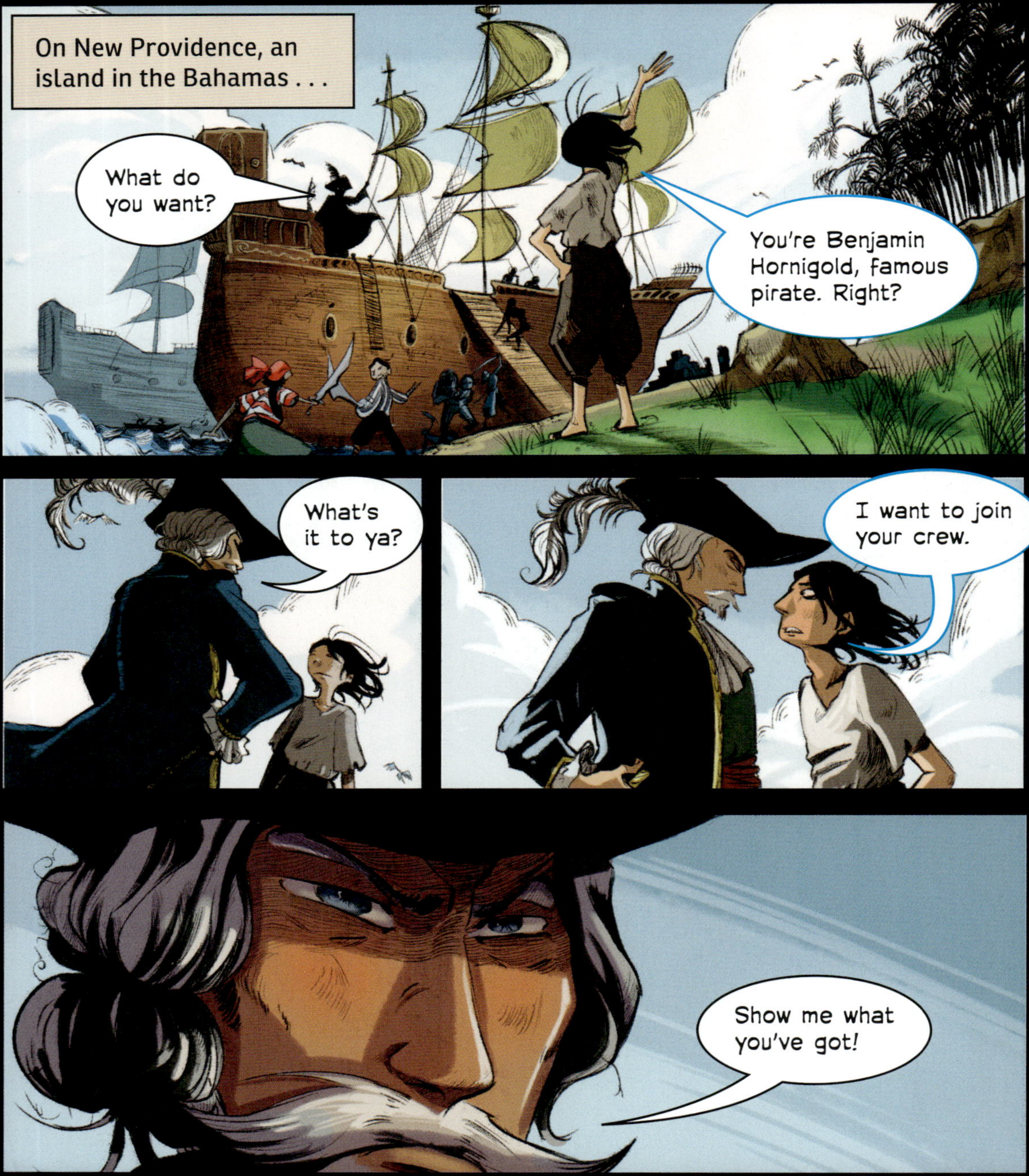
On New Providence, an island in the Bahamas . . .
What do you want?
You're Benjamin Hornigold, famous pirate. Right?
What's it to ya?
I want to join your crew.
Show me what you've got!

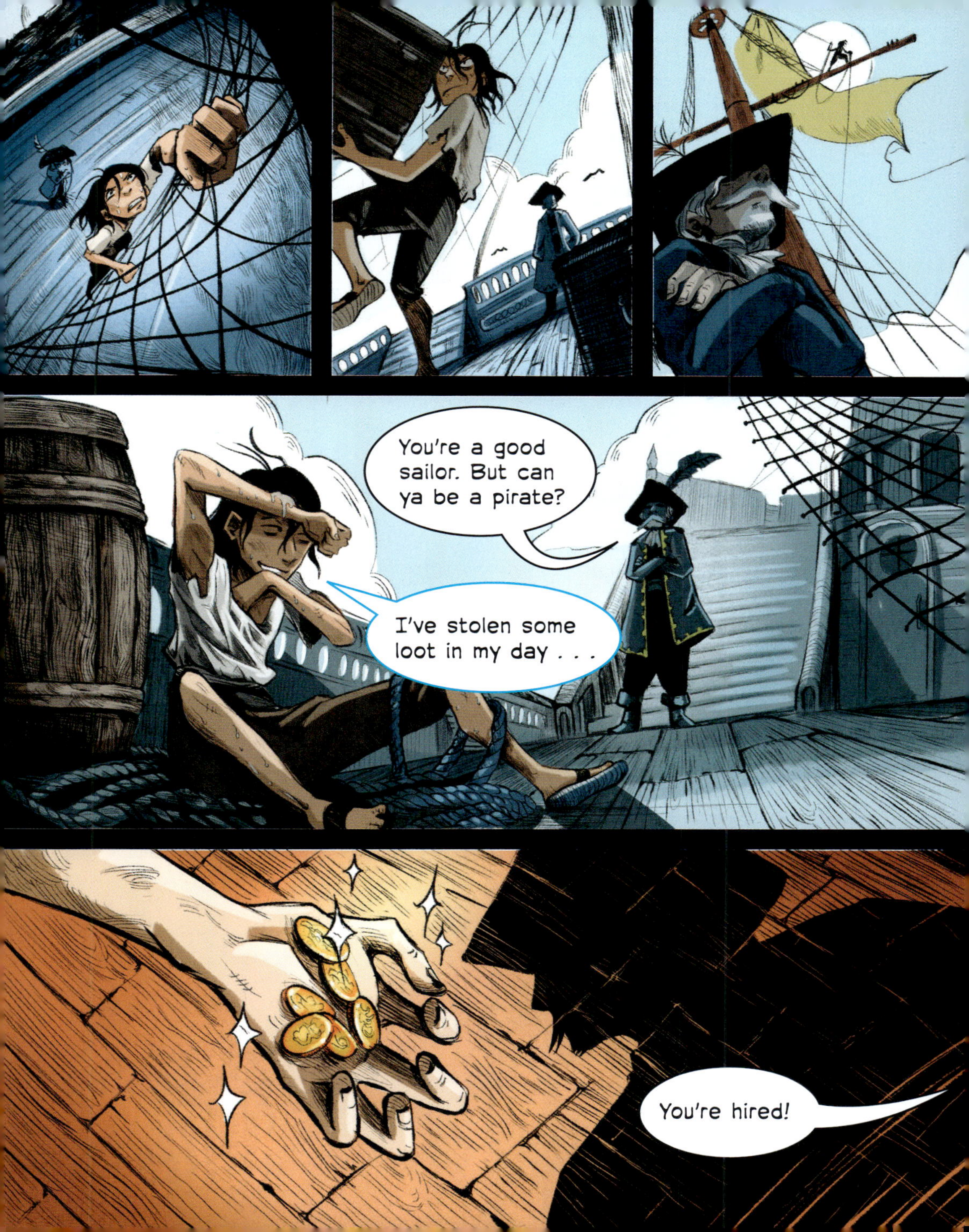
You're a good sailor. But can ya be a pirate?
I've stolen some loot in my day . . .
You're hired!

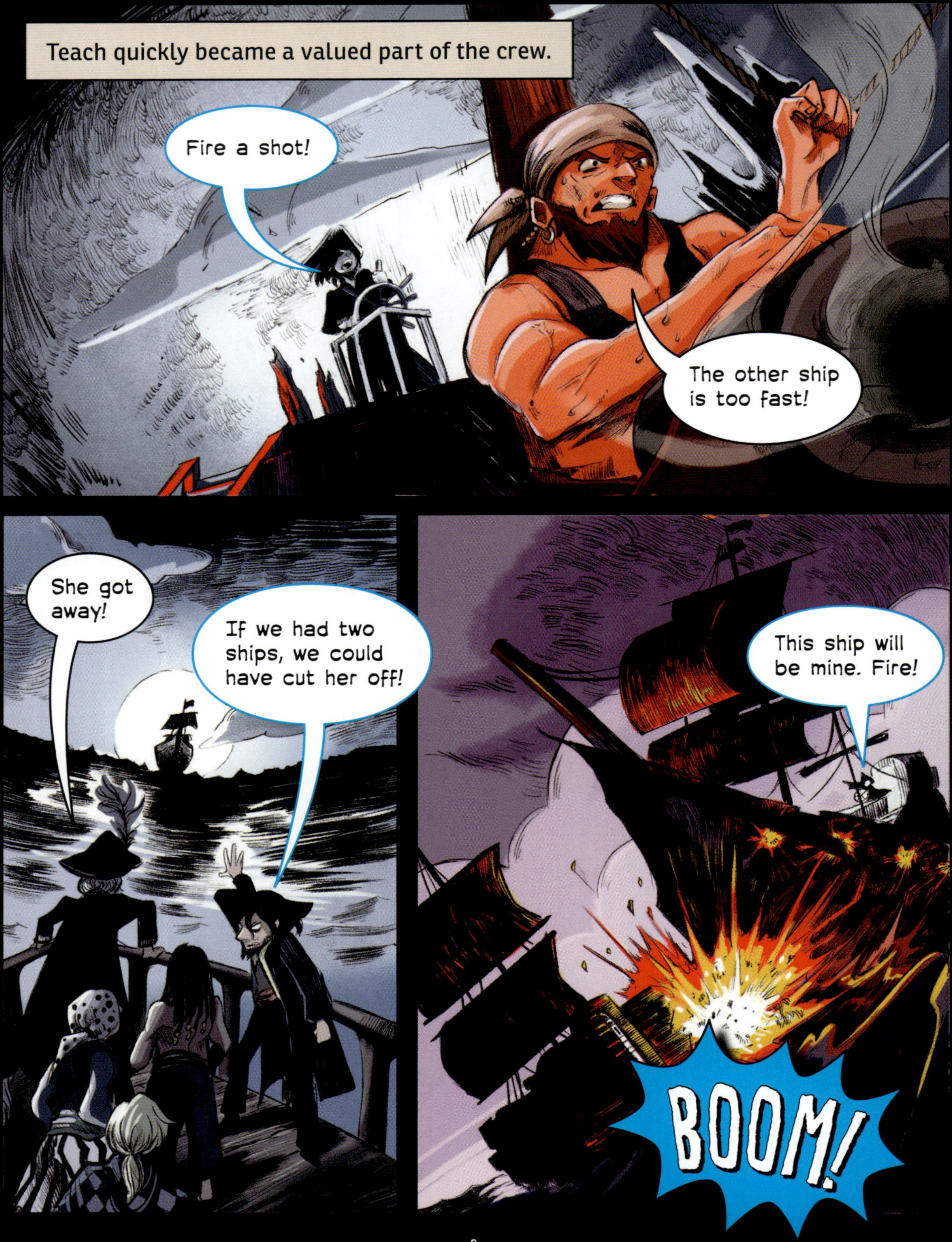
Teach quickly became a valued part of the crew.
Fire a shot!
The other ship is too fast!
She got away!
If we had two ships, we could have cut her off!
This ship will be mine. Fire!
BOOM!

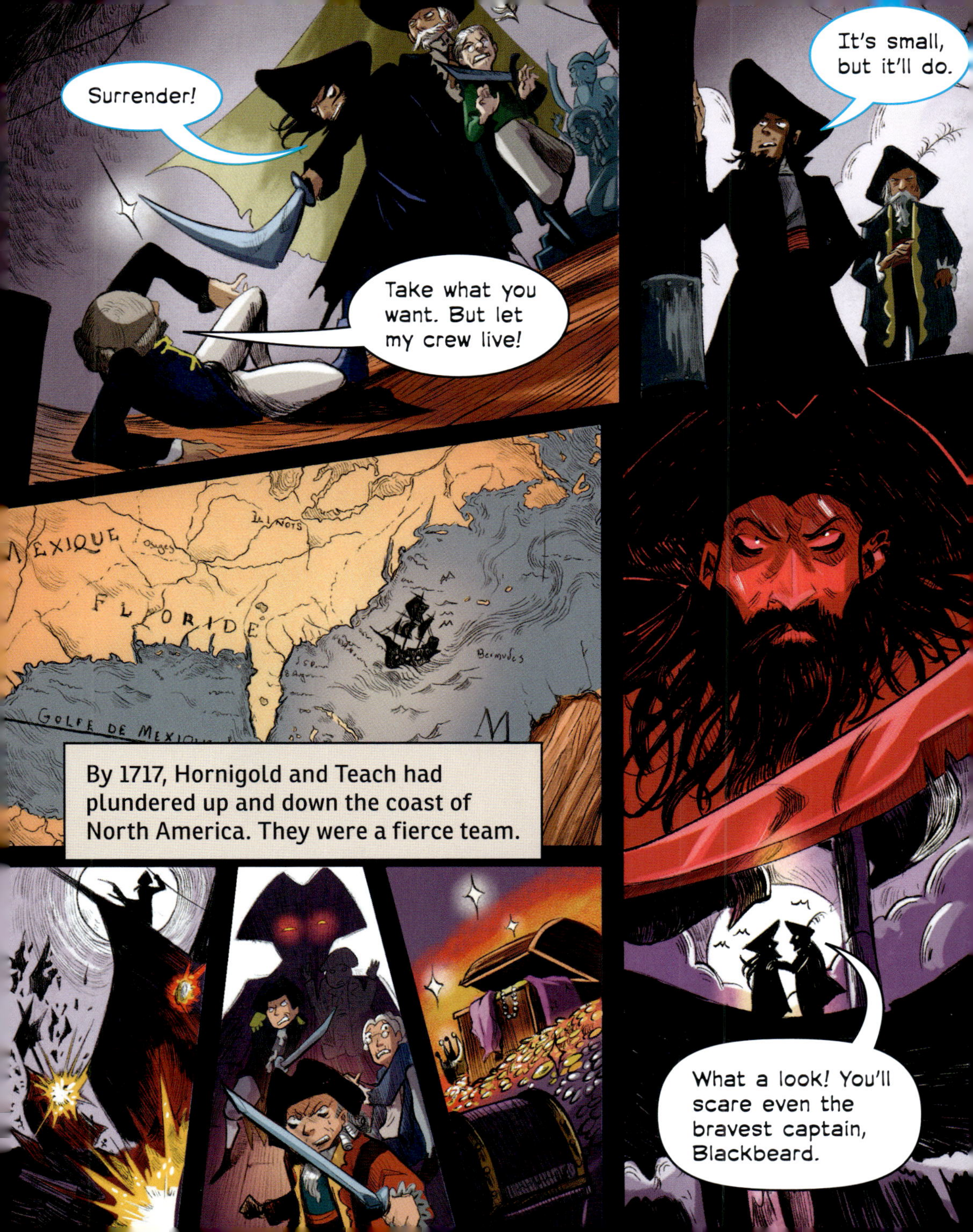
Surrender!
Take what you want. But let my crew live!
It's small, but it'll do.
FLORIDE
Bermudes
By 1717, Hornigold and Teach had plundered up and down the coast of North America. They were a fierce team.
What a look! You'll scare even the bravest captain, Blackbeard.

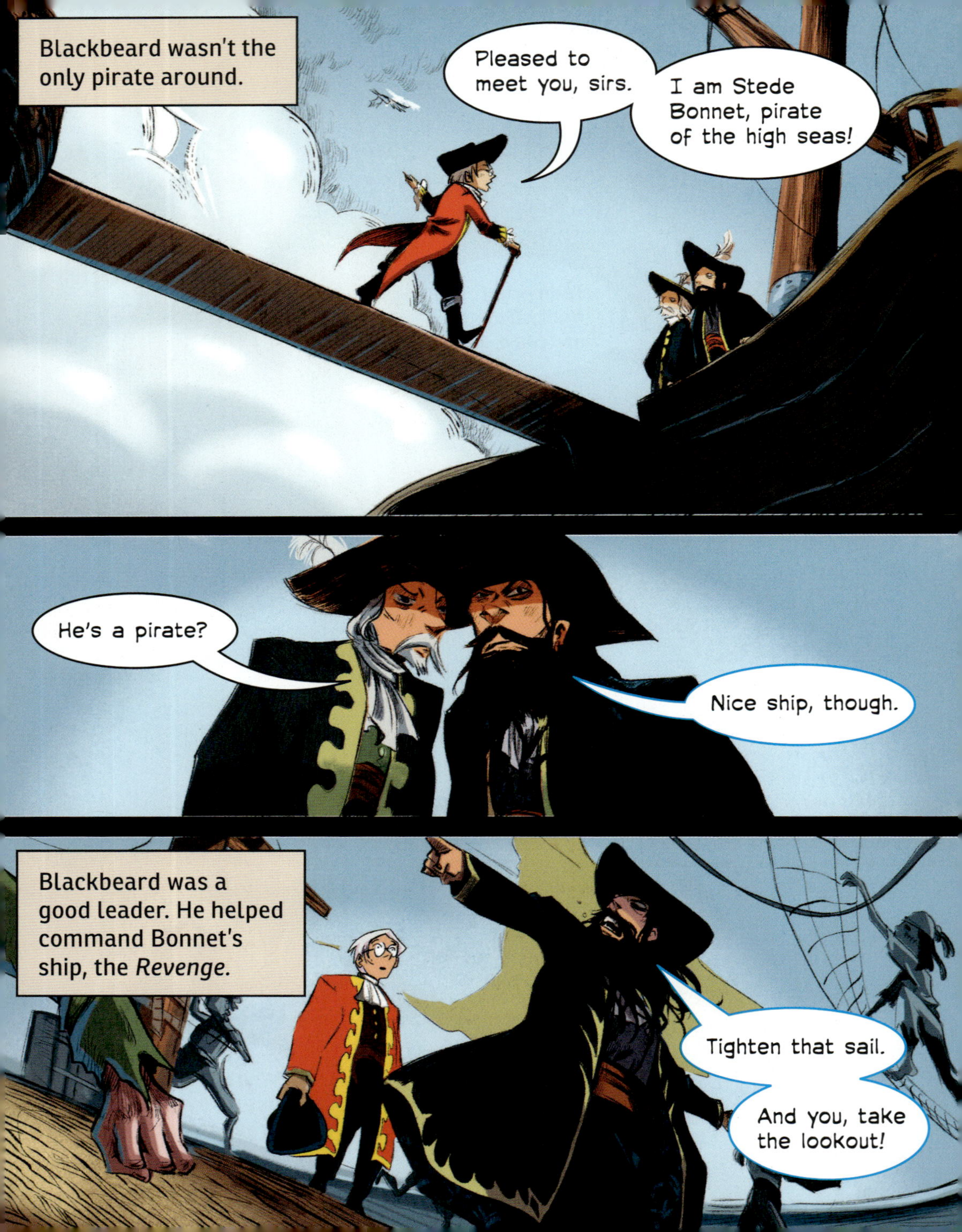

Blackbeard wasn't the only pirate around.
Pleased to meet you, sirs.
I am Stede Bonnet, pirate of the high seas!
He's a pirate?
Nice ship, though.
Blackbeard was a good leader. He helped command Bonnet's ship, the *Revenge*.
Tighten that sail.
And you, take the lookout!

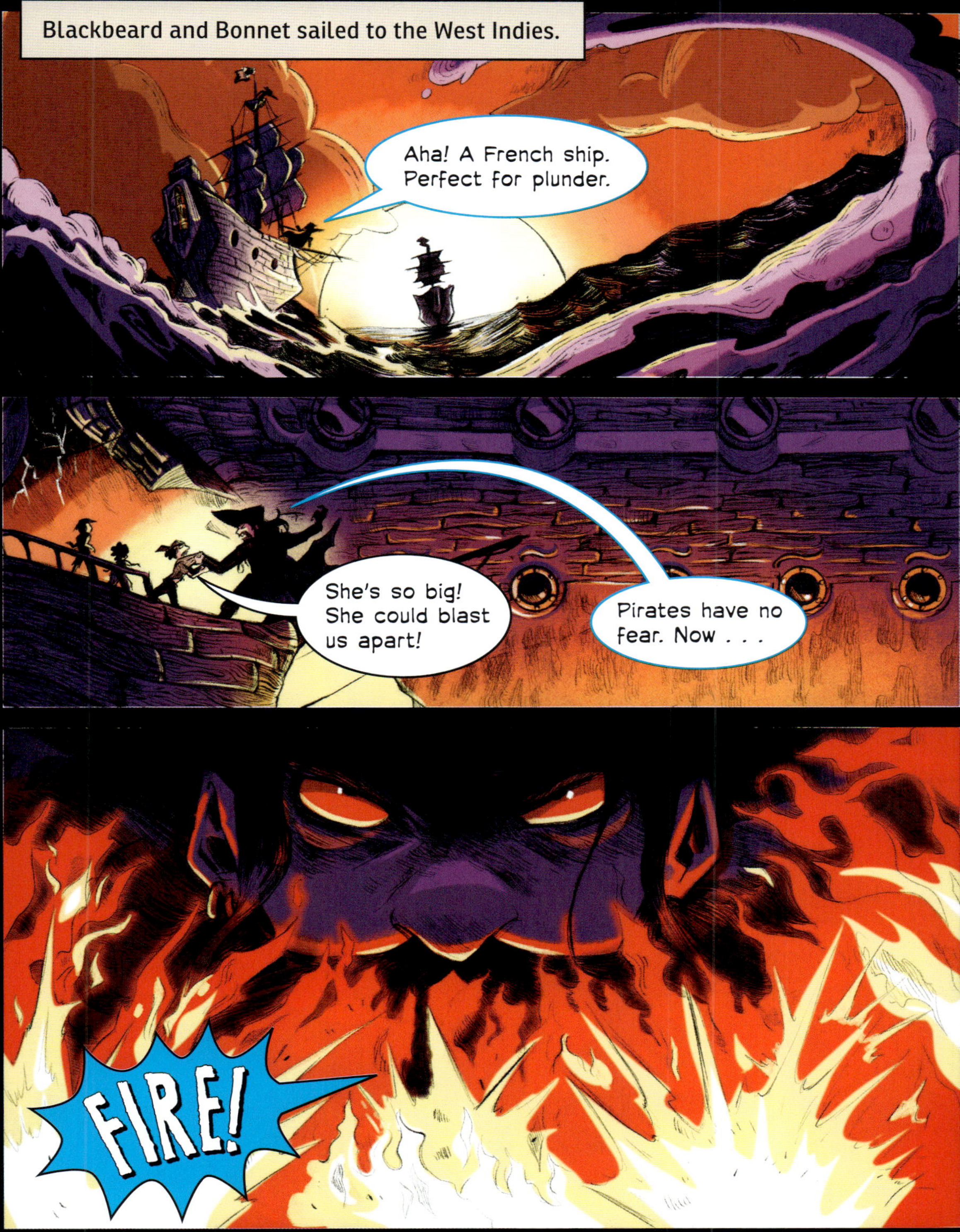
Blackbeard and Bonnet sailed to the West Indies.
Aha! A French ship. Perfect for plunder.
She's so big! She could blast us apart!
Pirates have no fear. Now . . .
FIRE!

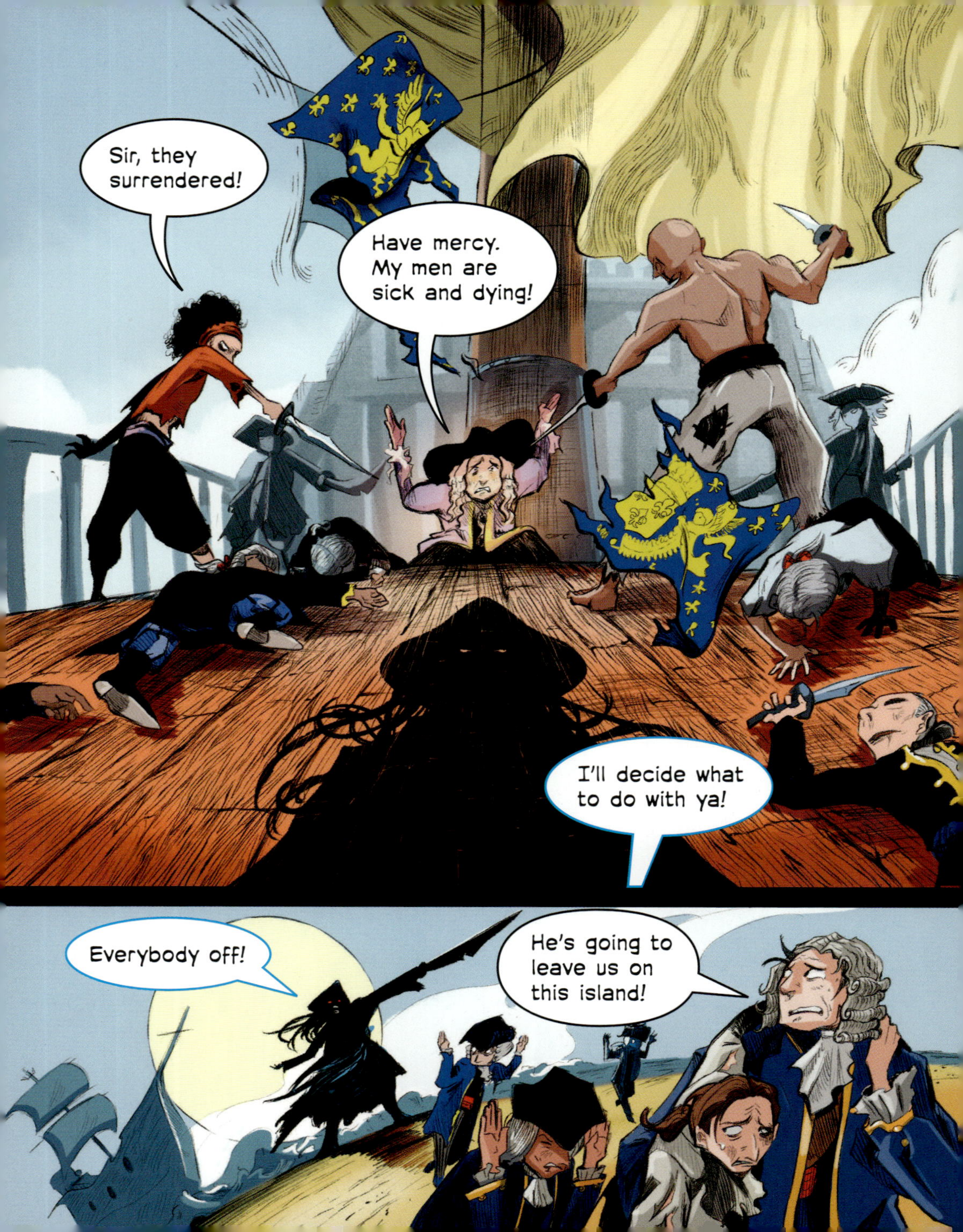
Sir, they surrendered!
Have mercy. My men are sick and dying!
I'll decide what to do with ya!
Everybody off!
He's going to leave us on this island!

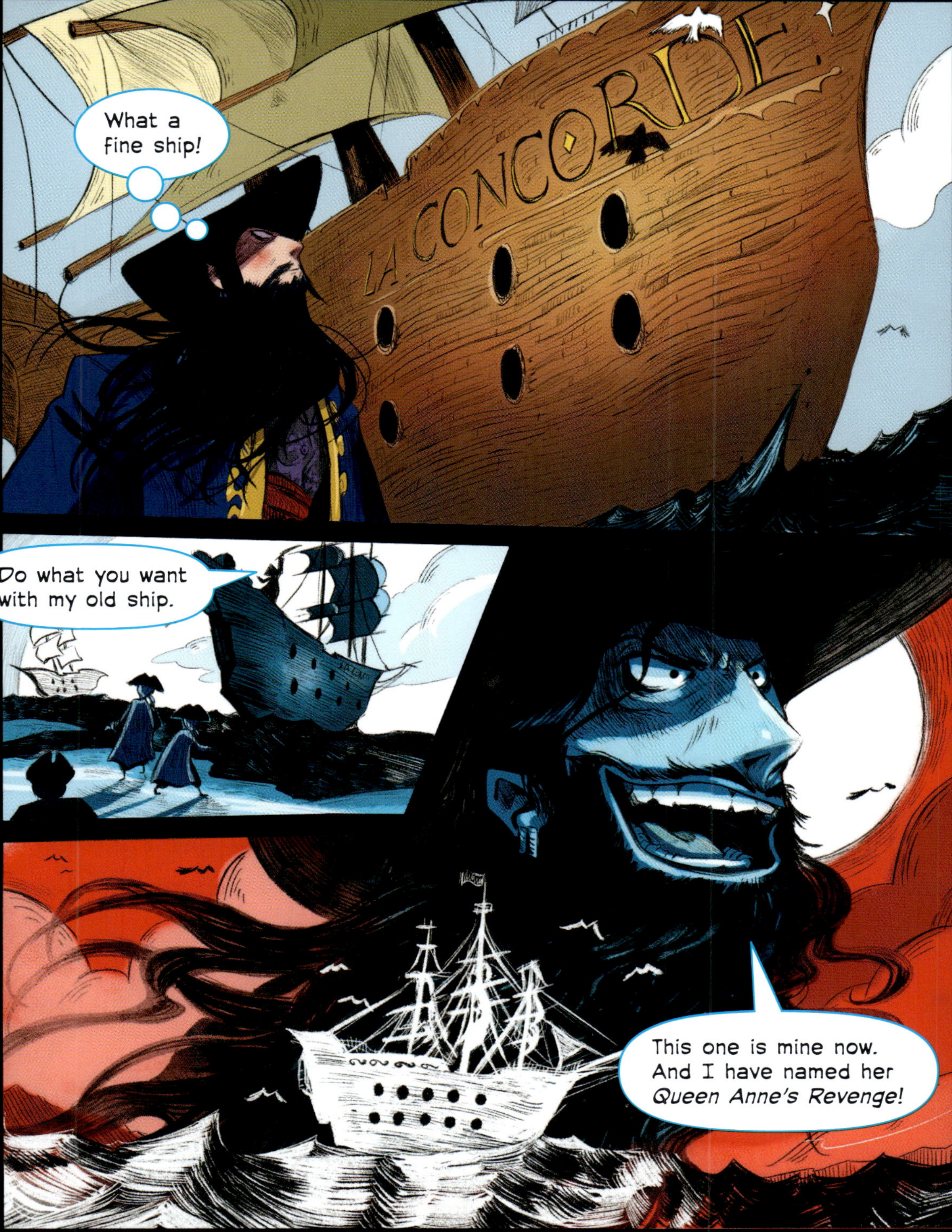
LA CONCORDE
What a fine ship!
Do what you want with my old ship.
This one is mine now. And I have named her *Queen Anne's Revenge*!

CHAPTER 2

NO MERCY!

In England, King George heard of the pirate problem in the American colonies.

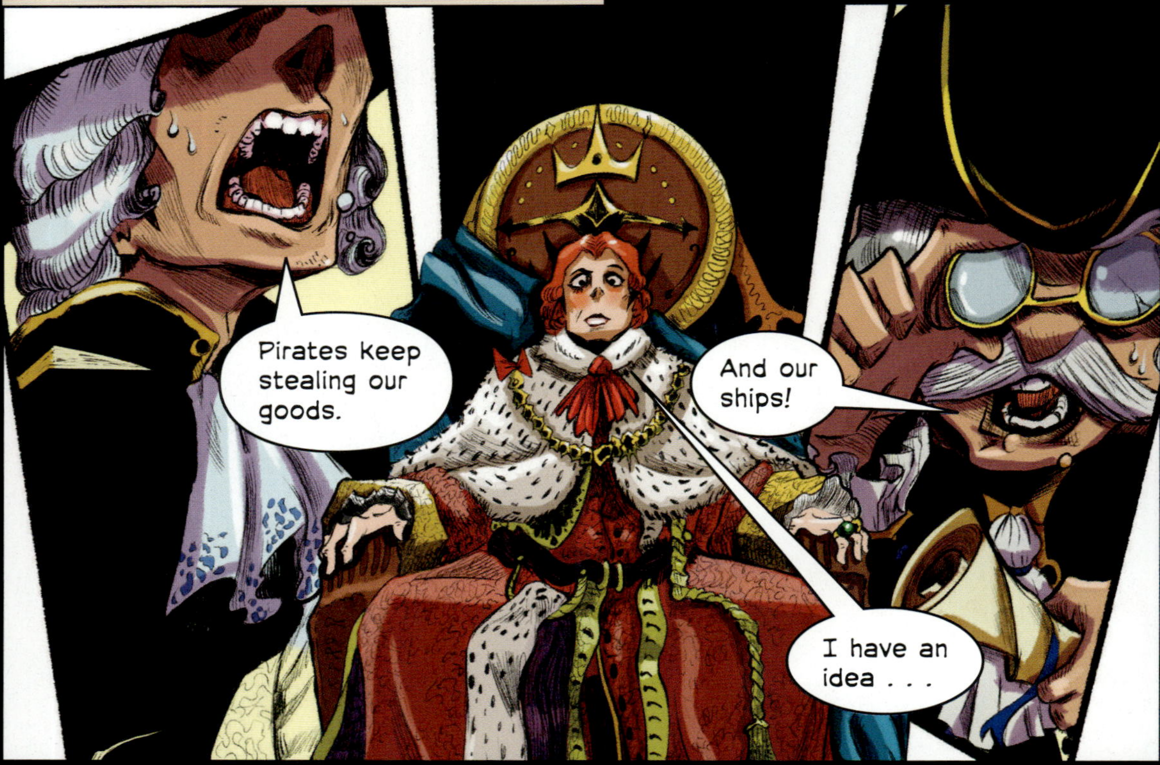
Pirates keep stealing our goods.
And our ships!
I have an idea . . .

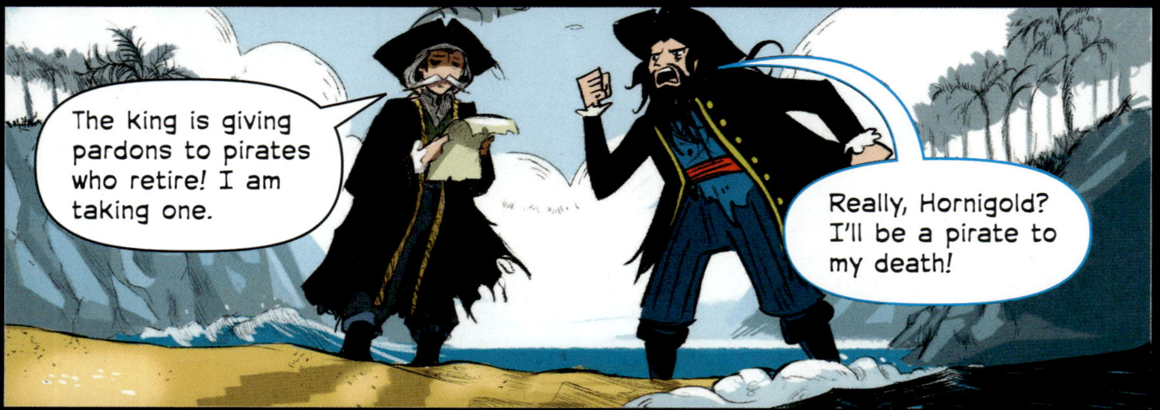
The king is giving pardons to pirates who retire! I am taking one.
Really, Hornigold? I'll be a pirate to my death!

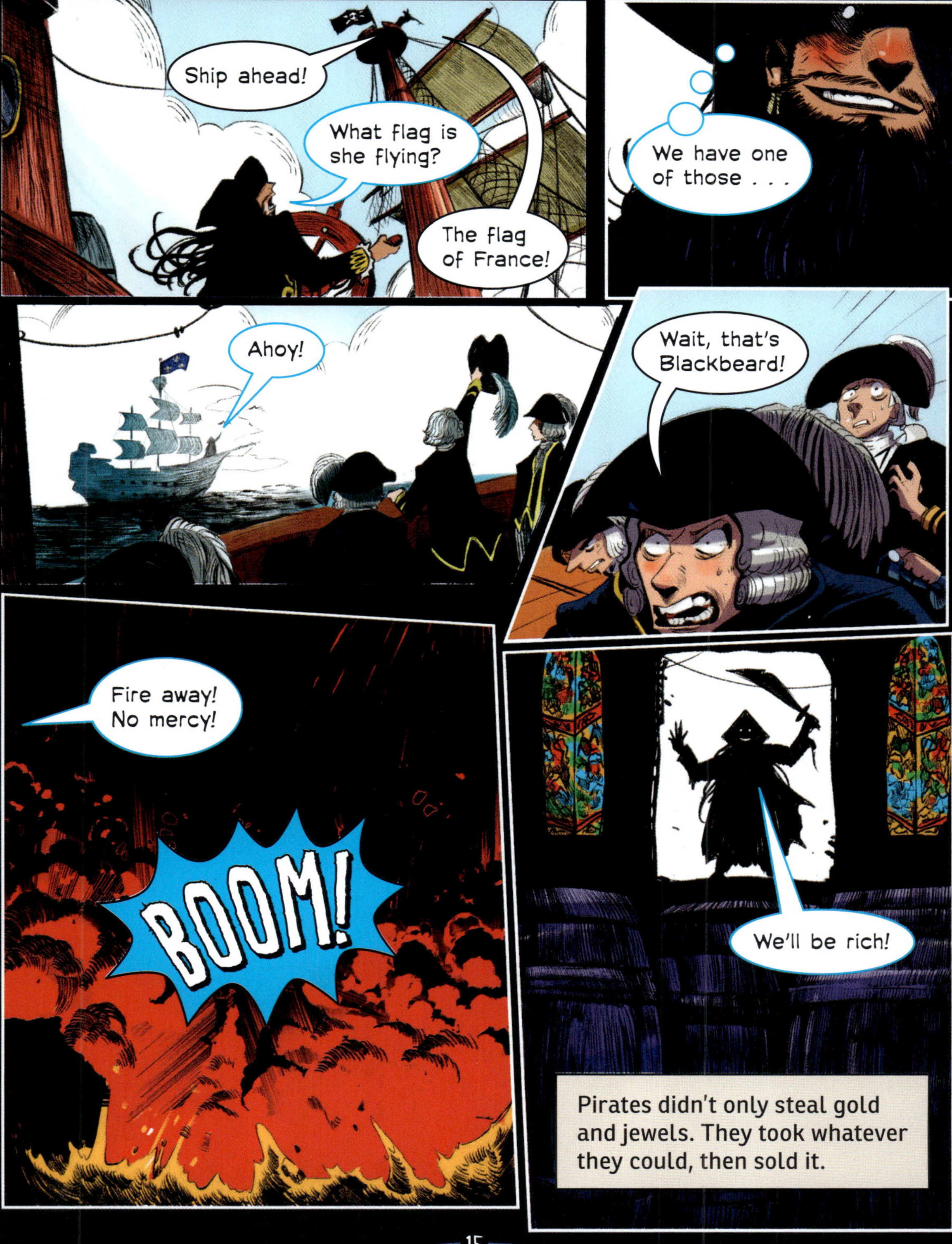
Ship ahead!
What flag is she flying?
The flag of France!
We have one of those . . .
Ahoy!
Wait, that's Blackbeard!
Fire away! No mercy!
BOOM!
We'll be rich!
Pirates didn't only steal gold and jewels. They took whatever they could, then sold it.

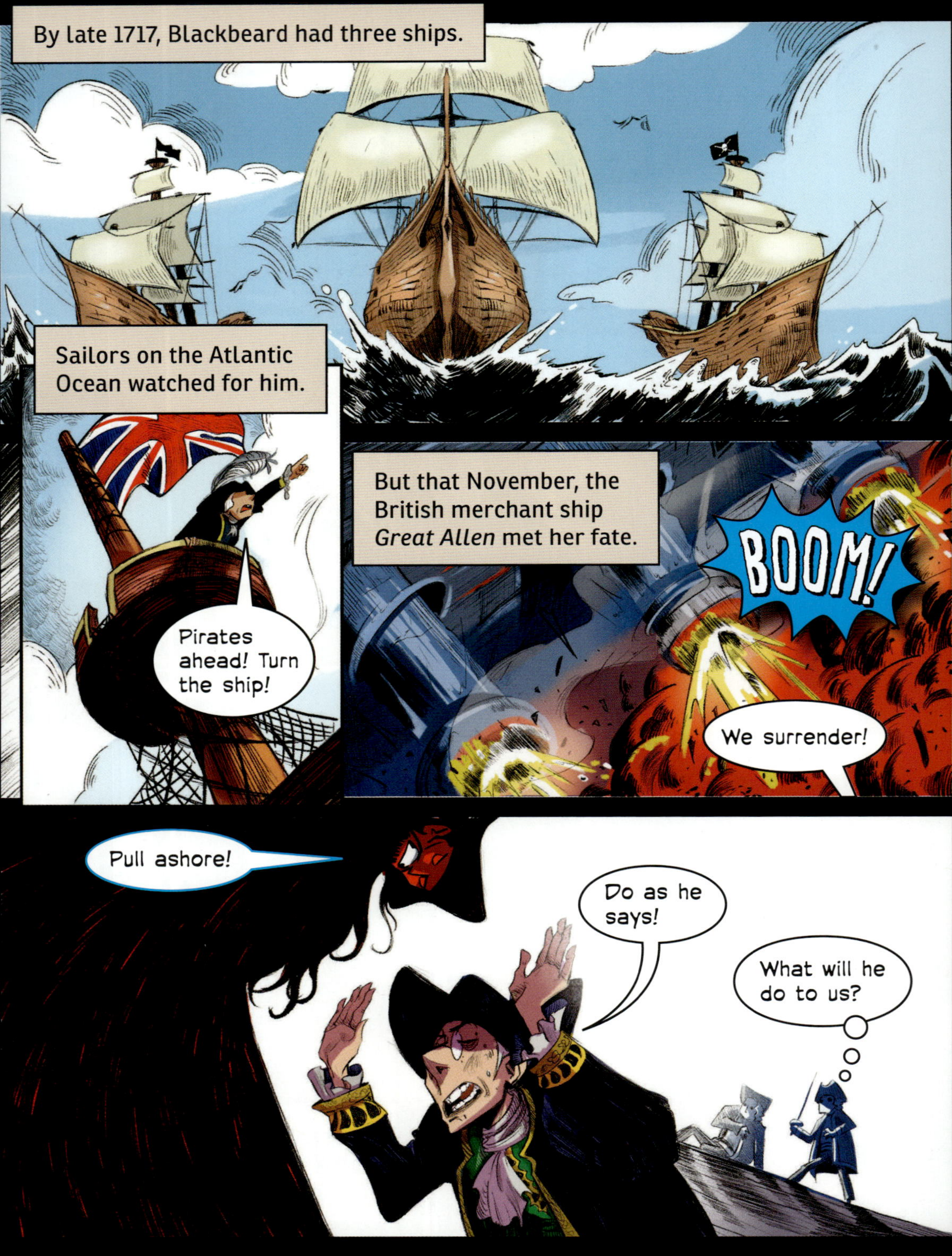

By late 1717, Blackbeard had three ships.
Sailors on the Atlantic Ocean watched for him.
Pirates ahead! Turn the ship!
But that November, the British merchant ship *Great Allen* met her fate.
BOOM!
We surrender!
Pull ashore!
Do as he says!
What will he do to us?

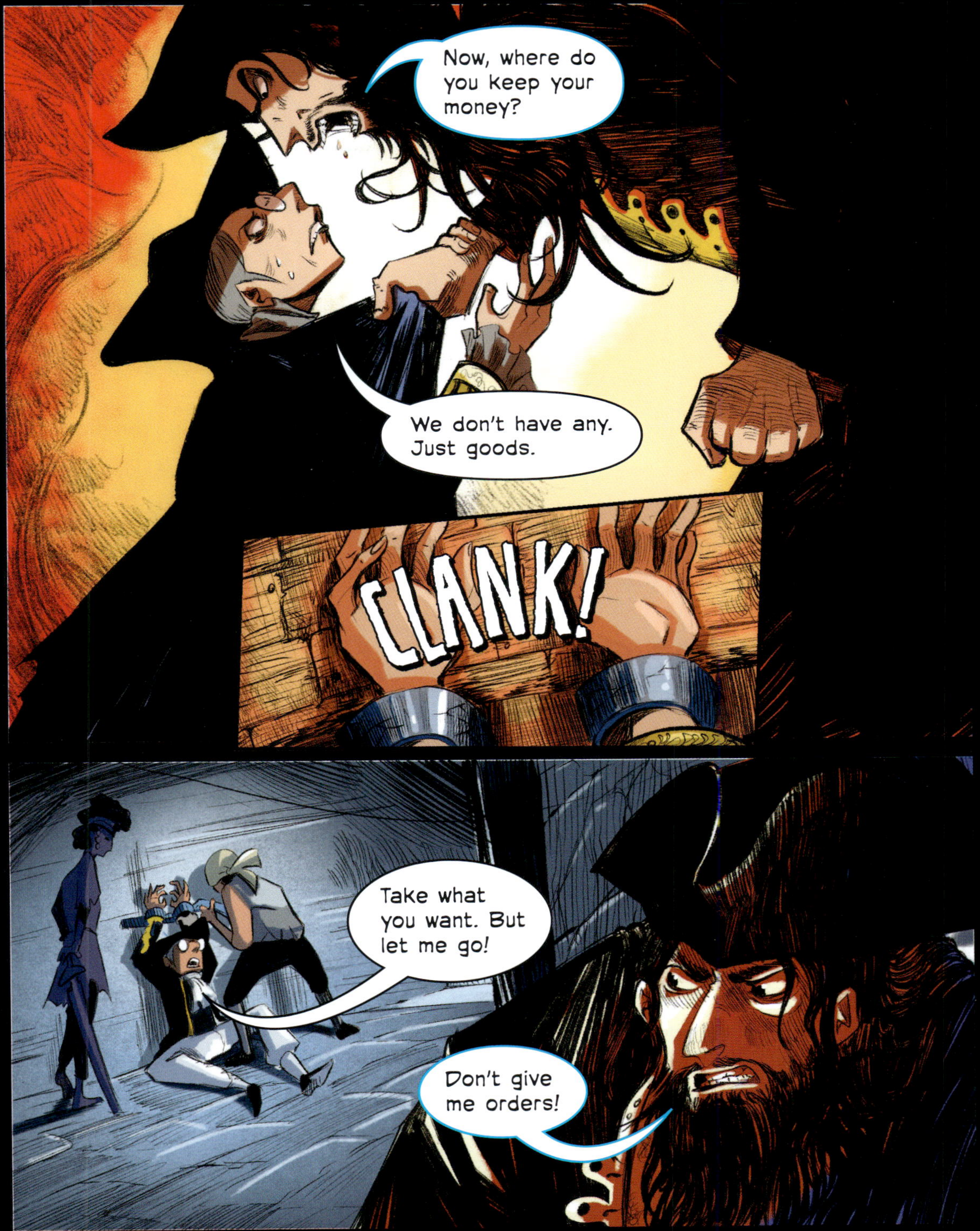
Now, where do you keep your money?
We don't have any. Just goods.
CLANK!
Take what you want. But let me go!
Don't give me orders!

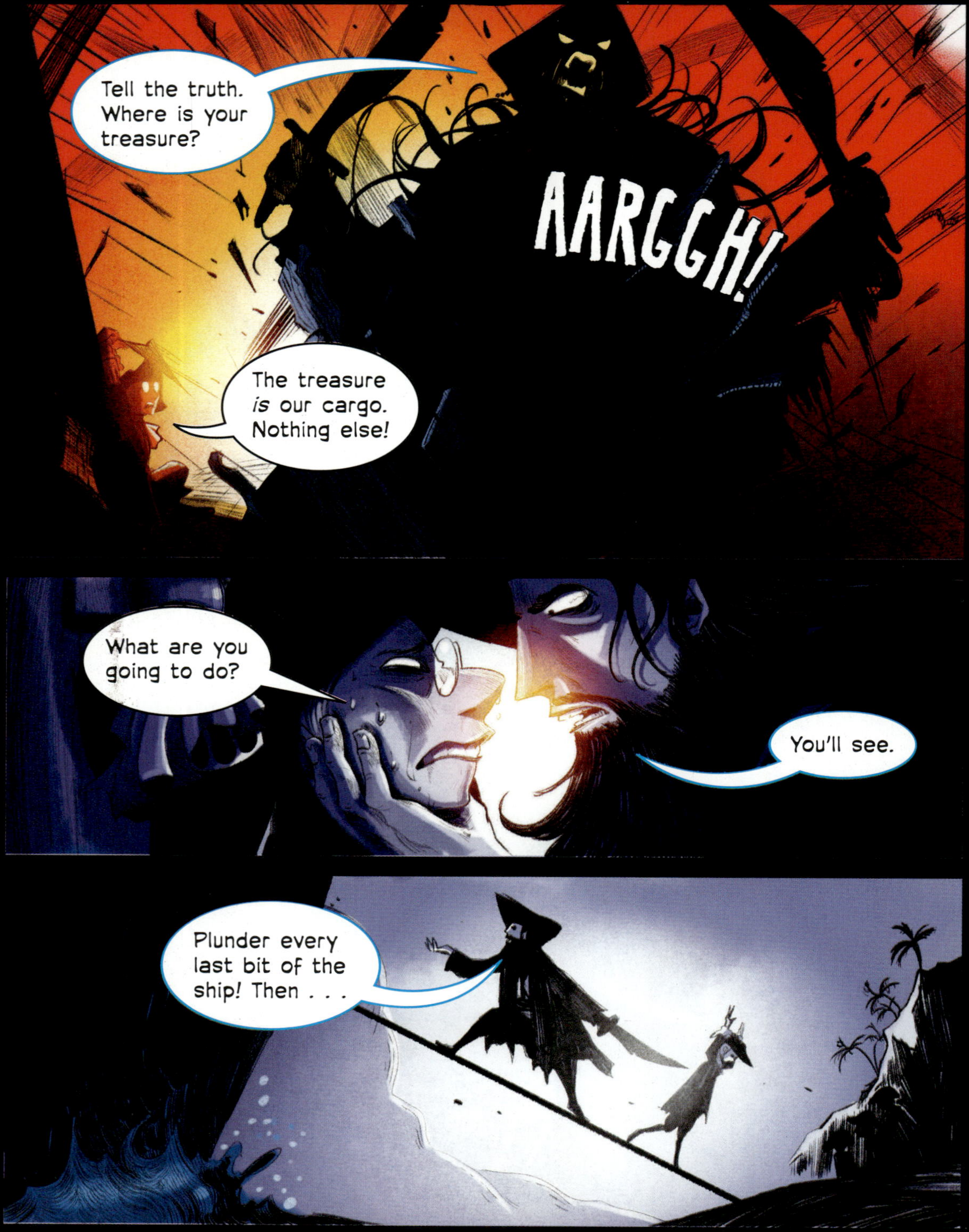
Tell the truth. Where is your treasure?
AARGGH!
The treasure *is* our cargo. Nothing else!
What are you going to do?
You'll see.
Plunder every last bit of the ship! Then . . .

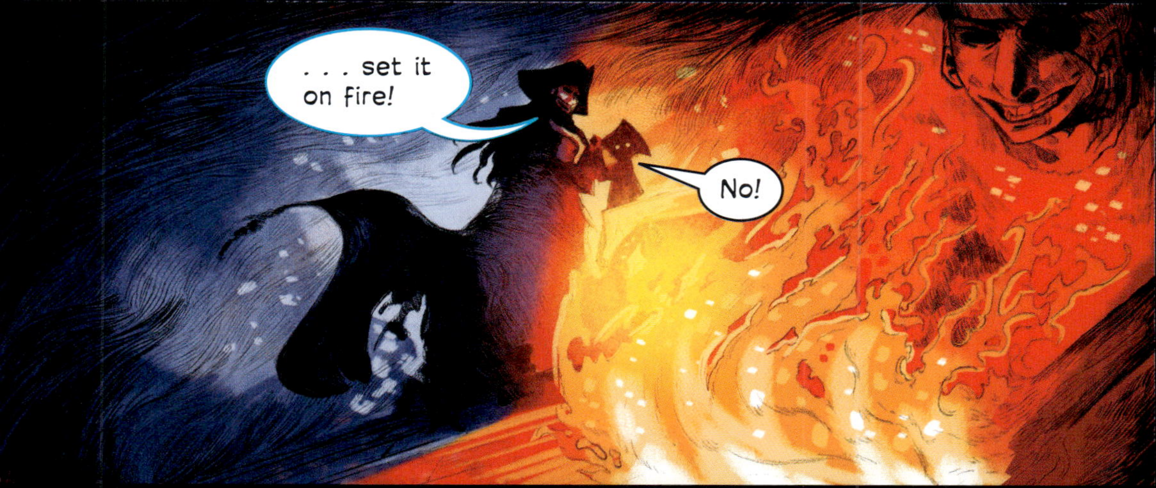
. . . set it on fire!
No!

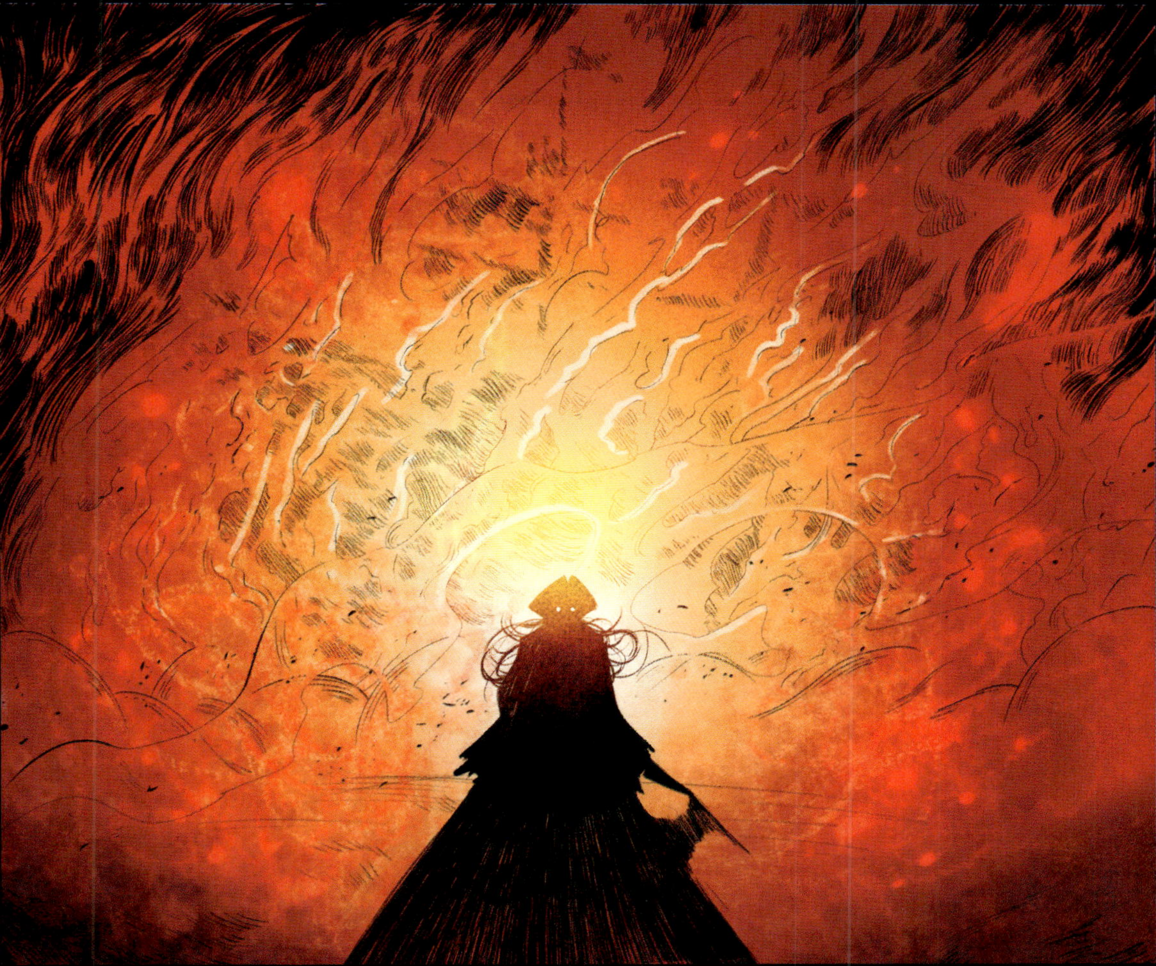

CHAPTER 3

PIRATE PROBLEM

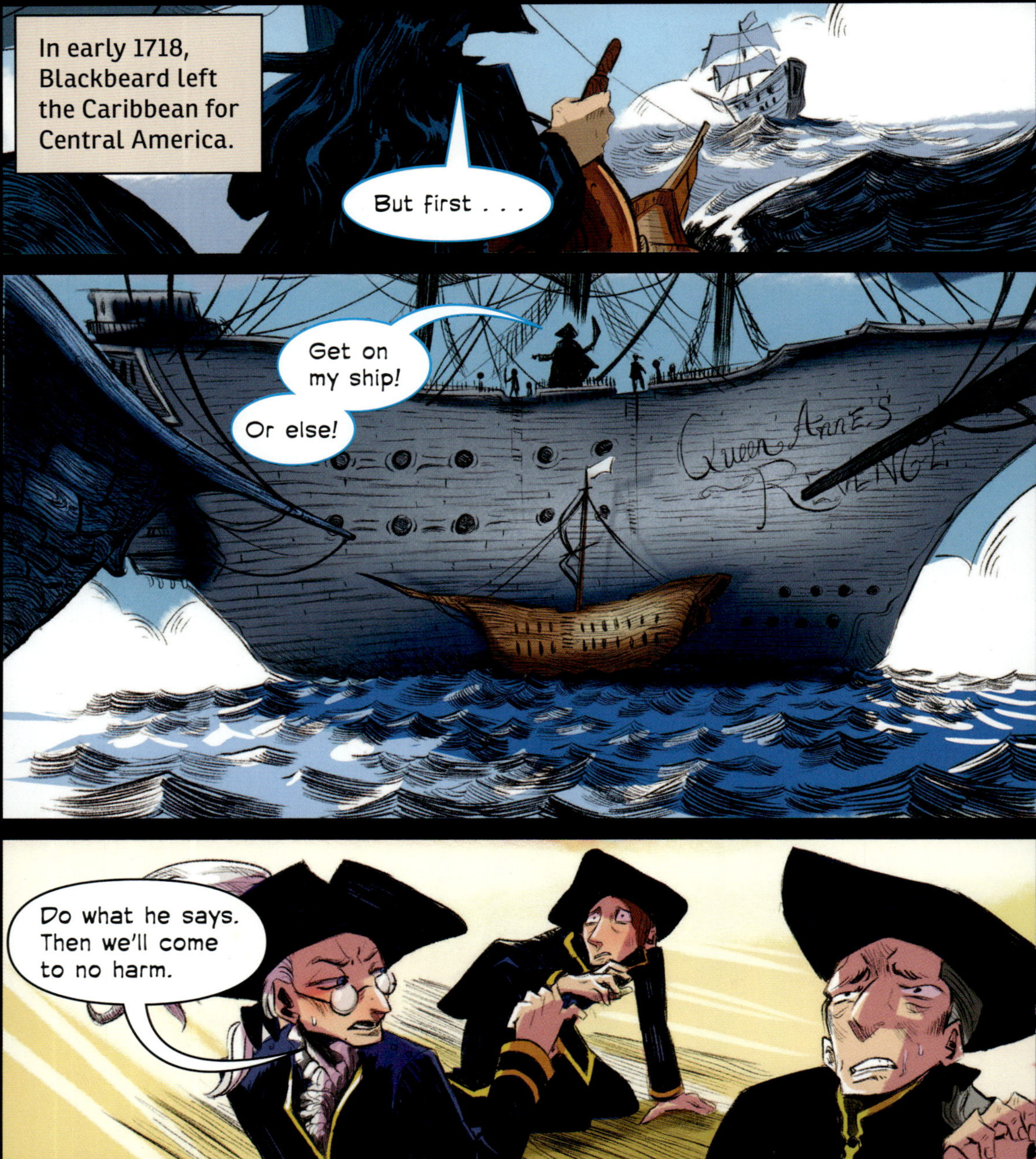

In early 1718, Blackbeard left the Caribbean for Central America.
But first . . .
Get on my ship!
Or else!
Do what he says. Then we'll come to no harm.

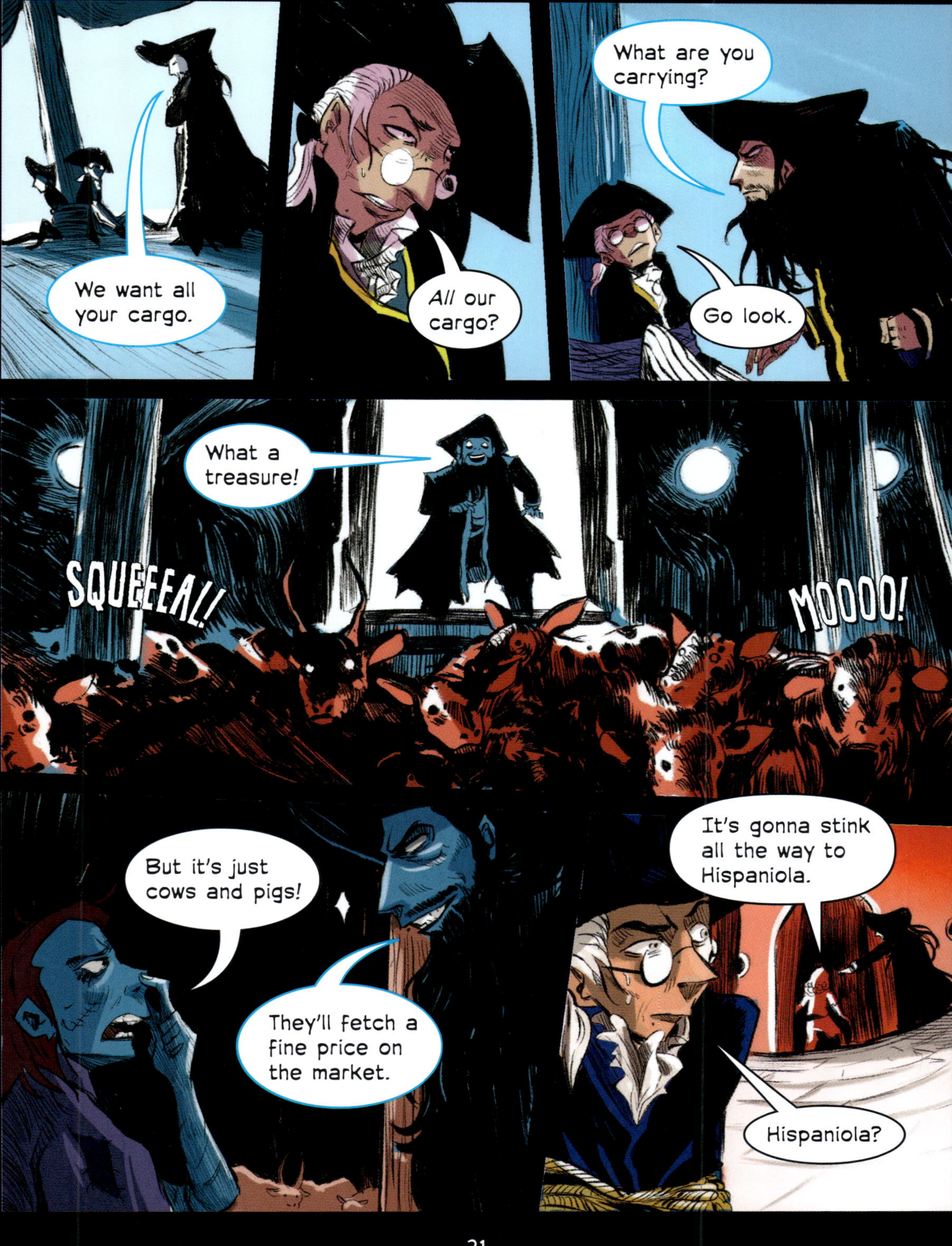
We want all your cargo.
All our cargo?
What are you carrying?
Go look.
What a treasure!
SQUEEEAL!
MOOOO!
But it's just cows and pigs!
They'll fetch a fine price on the market.
It's gonna stink all the way to Hispaniola.
Hispaniola?

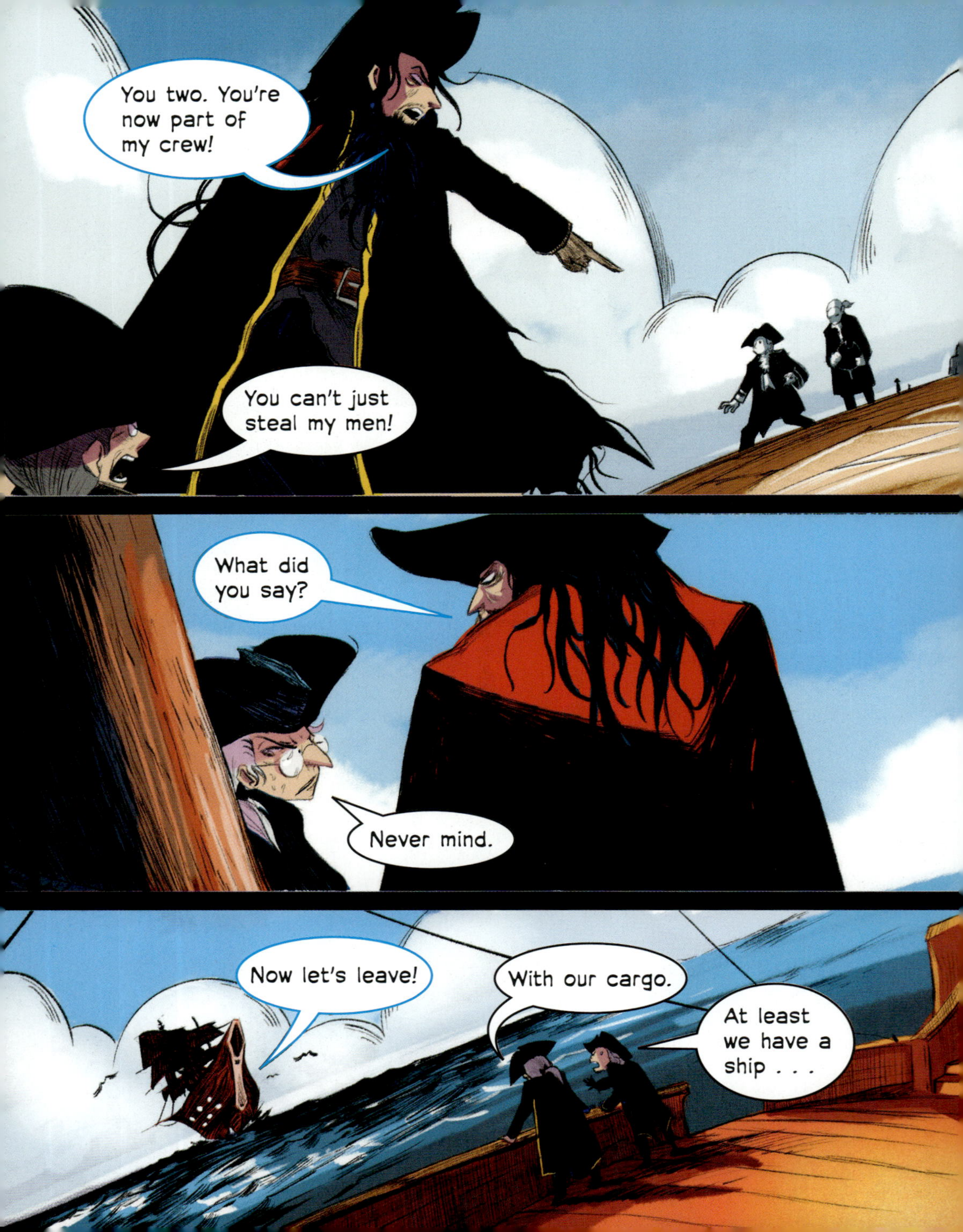
You two. You're now part of my crew!
You can't just steal my men!
What did you say?
Never mind.
Now let's leave!
With our cargo.
At least we have a ship . . .

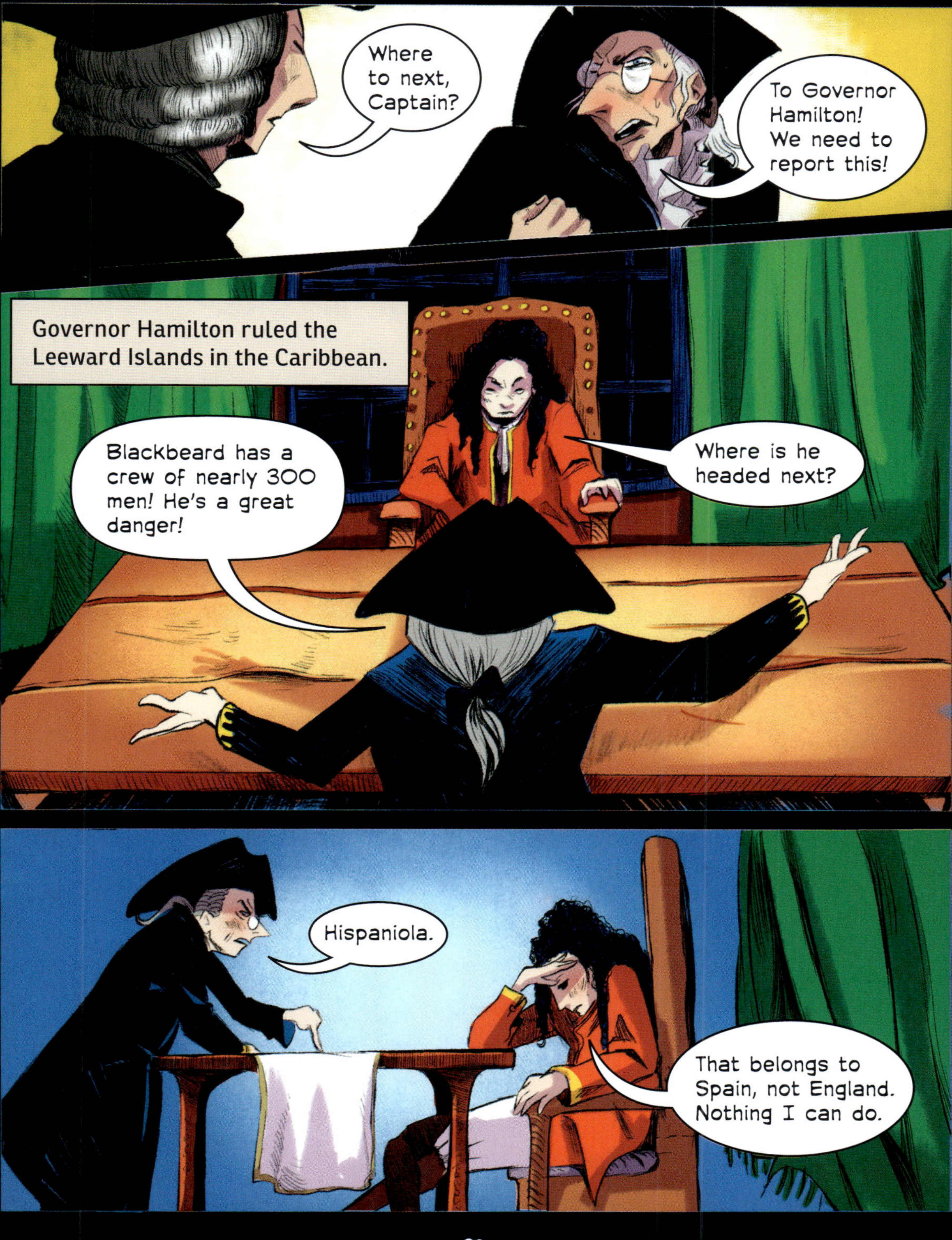
Where to next, Captain?
To Governor Hamilton! We need to report this!
Governor Hamilton ruled the Leeward Islands in the Caribbean.
Where is he headed next?
Blackbeard has a crew of nearly 300 men! He's a great danger!
Hispaniola.
That belongs to Spain, not England. Nothing I can do.

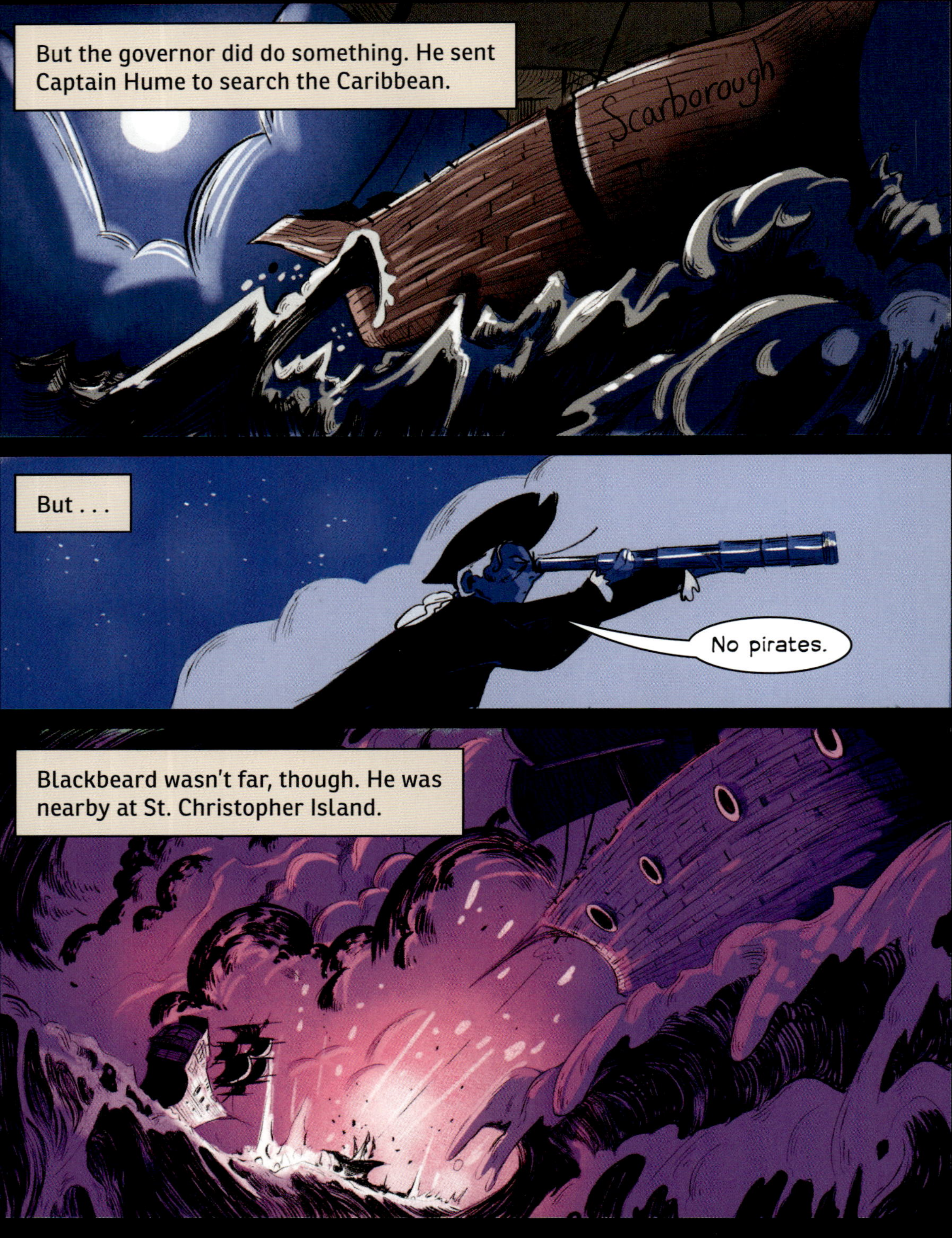
But the governor did do something. He sent Captain Hume to search the Caribbean.
Scarborough
But . . .
No pirates.
Blackbeard wasn't far, though. He was nearby at St. Christopher Island.

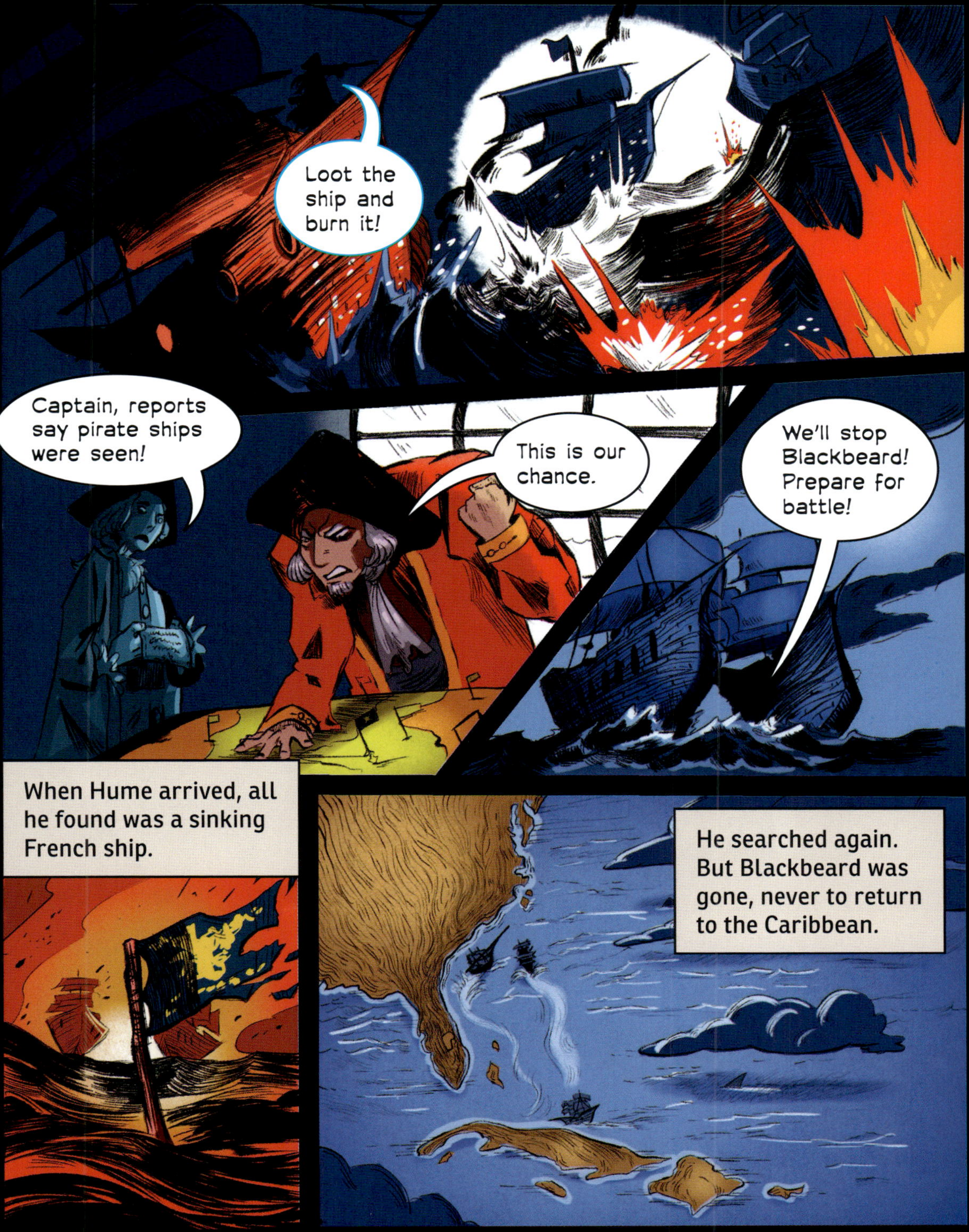
Loot the ship and burn it!
Captain, reports say pirate ships were seen!
This is our chance.
We'll stop Blackbeard! Prepare for battle!
When Hume arrived, all he found was a sinking French ship.
He searched again. But Blackbeard was gone, never to return to the Caribbean.

CHAPTER 4

RAIDS AND RANSOM

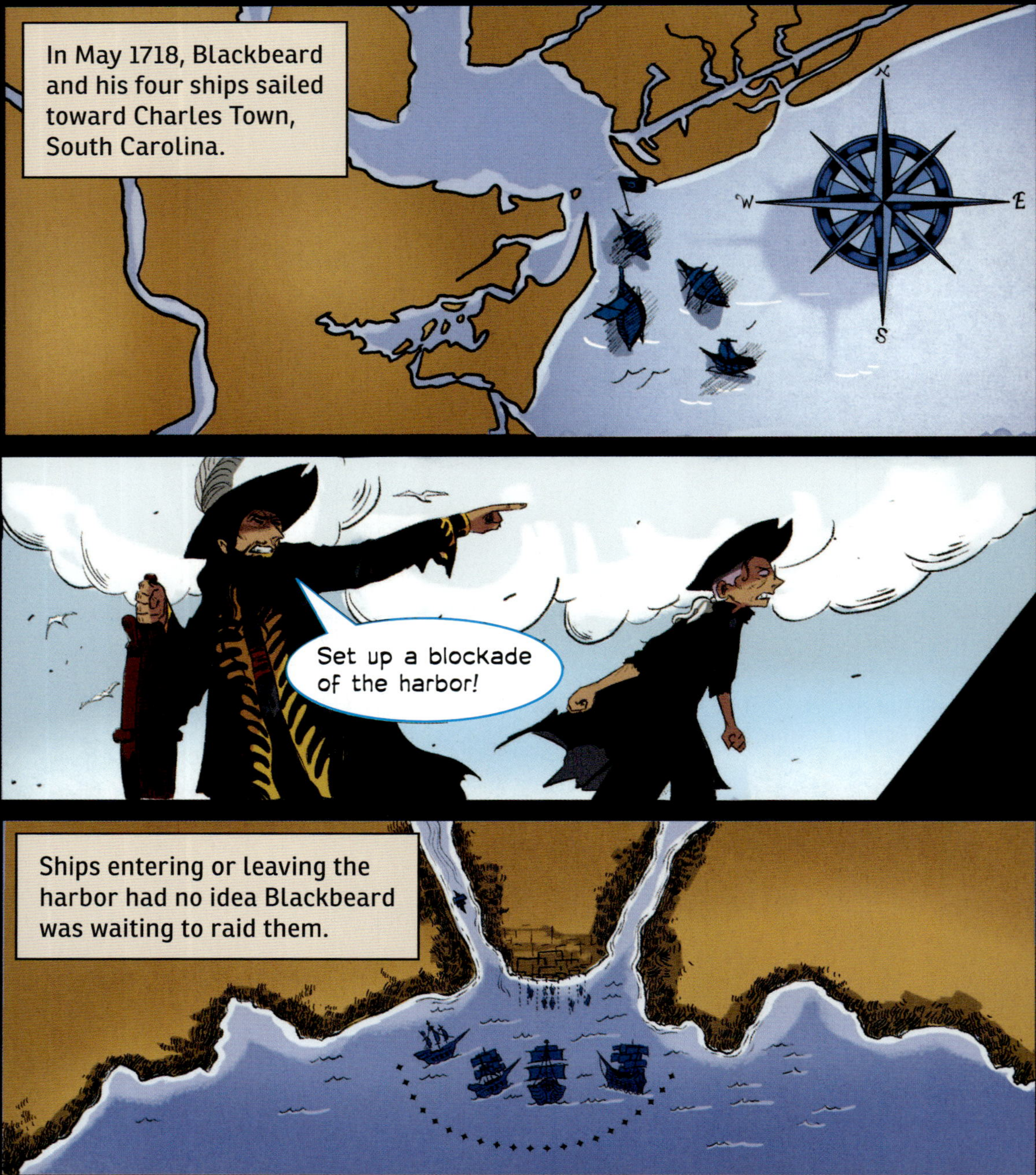
In May 1718, Blackbeard and his four ships sailed toward Charles Town, South Carolina.
N
W
E
S
Set up a blockade of the harbor!
Ships entering or leaving the harbor had no idea Blackbeard was waiting to raid them.

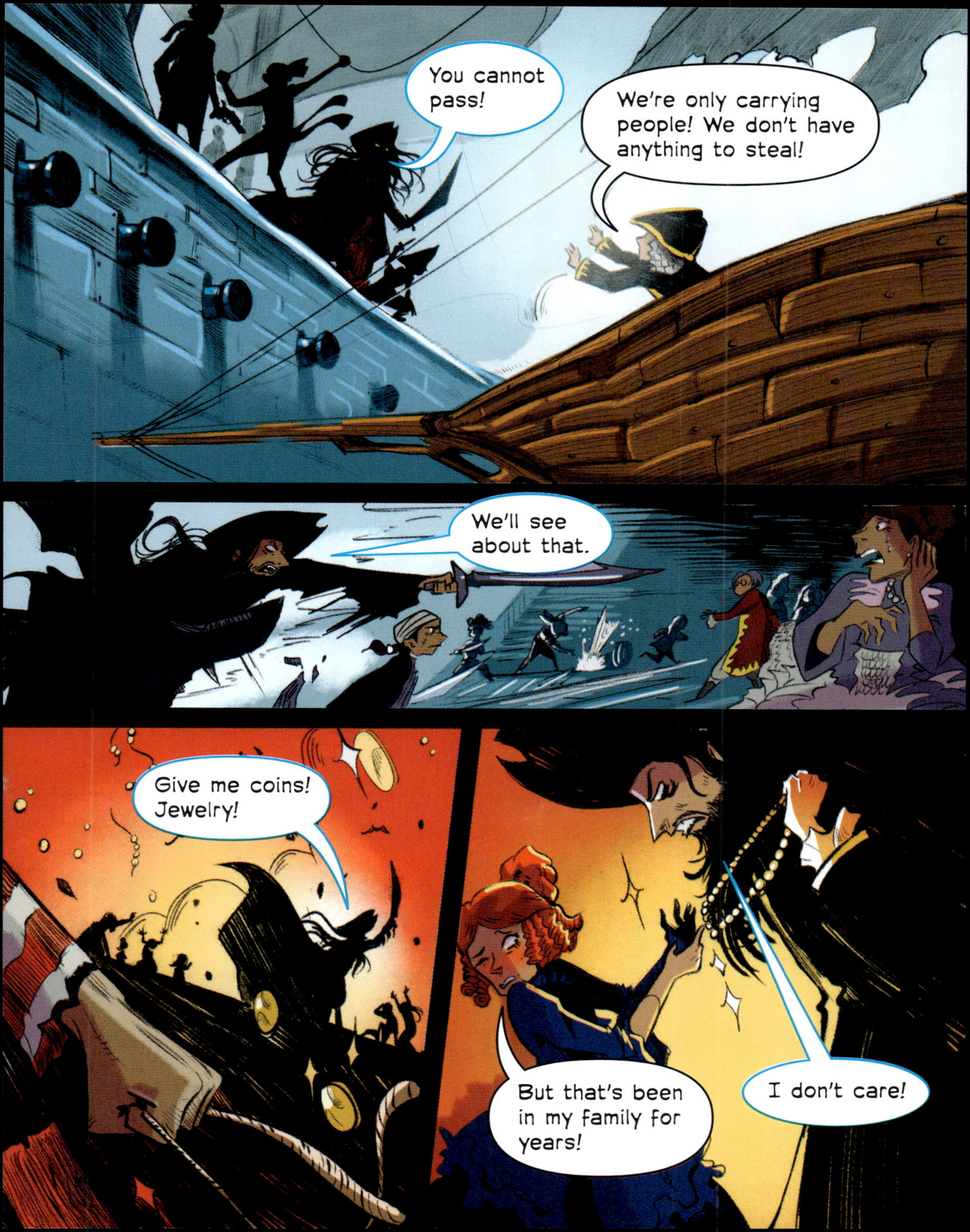
You cannot pass!
We're only carrying people! We don't have anything to steal!
We'll see about that.
Give me coins! Jewelry!
But that's been in my family for years!
I don't care!

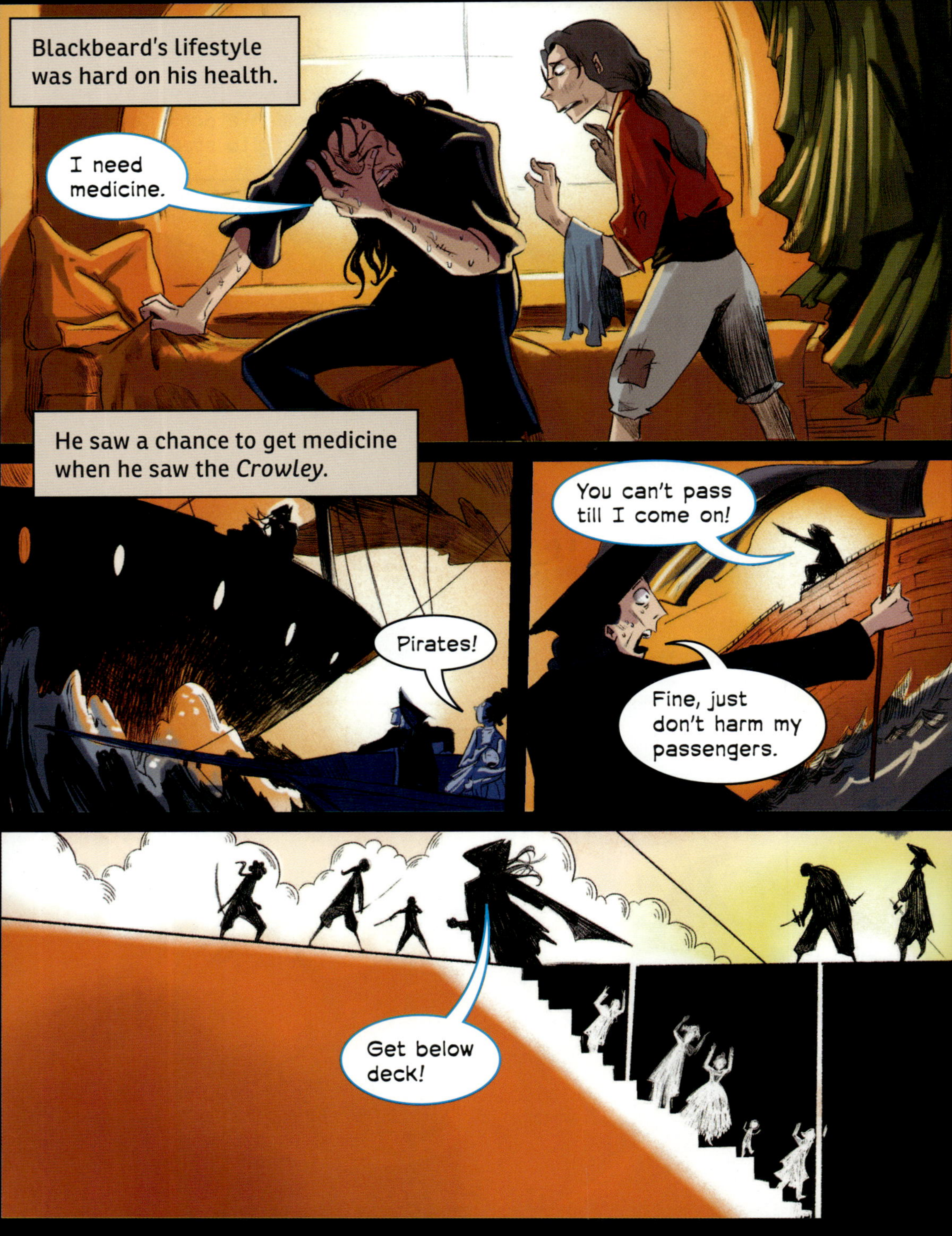
Blackbeard's lifestyle was hard on his health.
I need medicine.
He saw a chance to get medicine when he saw the *Crowley*.
Pirates!
You can't pass till I come on!
Fine, just don't harm my passengers.
Get below deck!

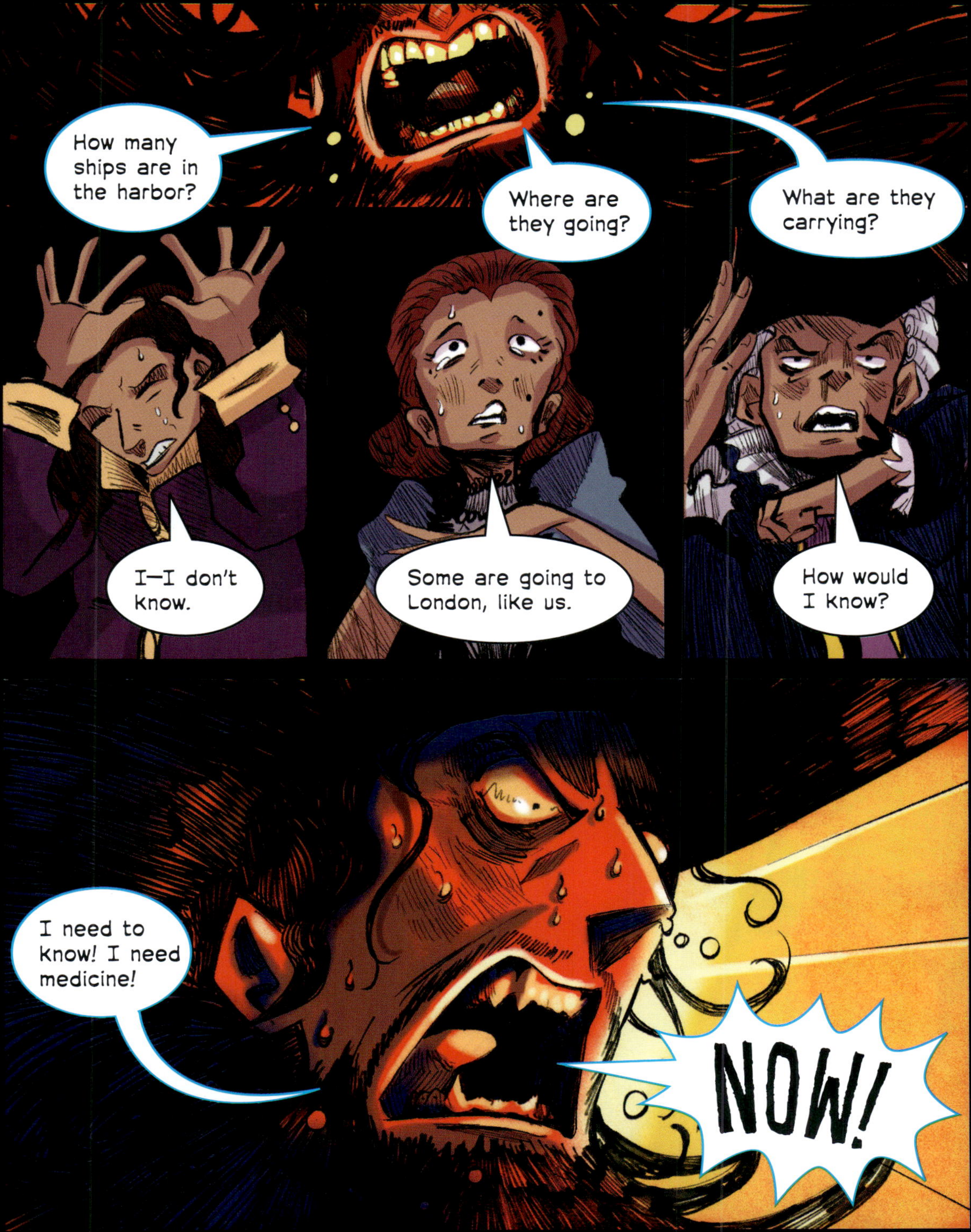
How many ships are in the harbor?
Where are they going?
What are they carrying?
I—I don't know.
Some are going to London, like us.
How would I know?
I need to know! I need medicine!
NOW!

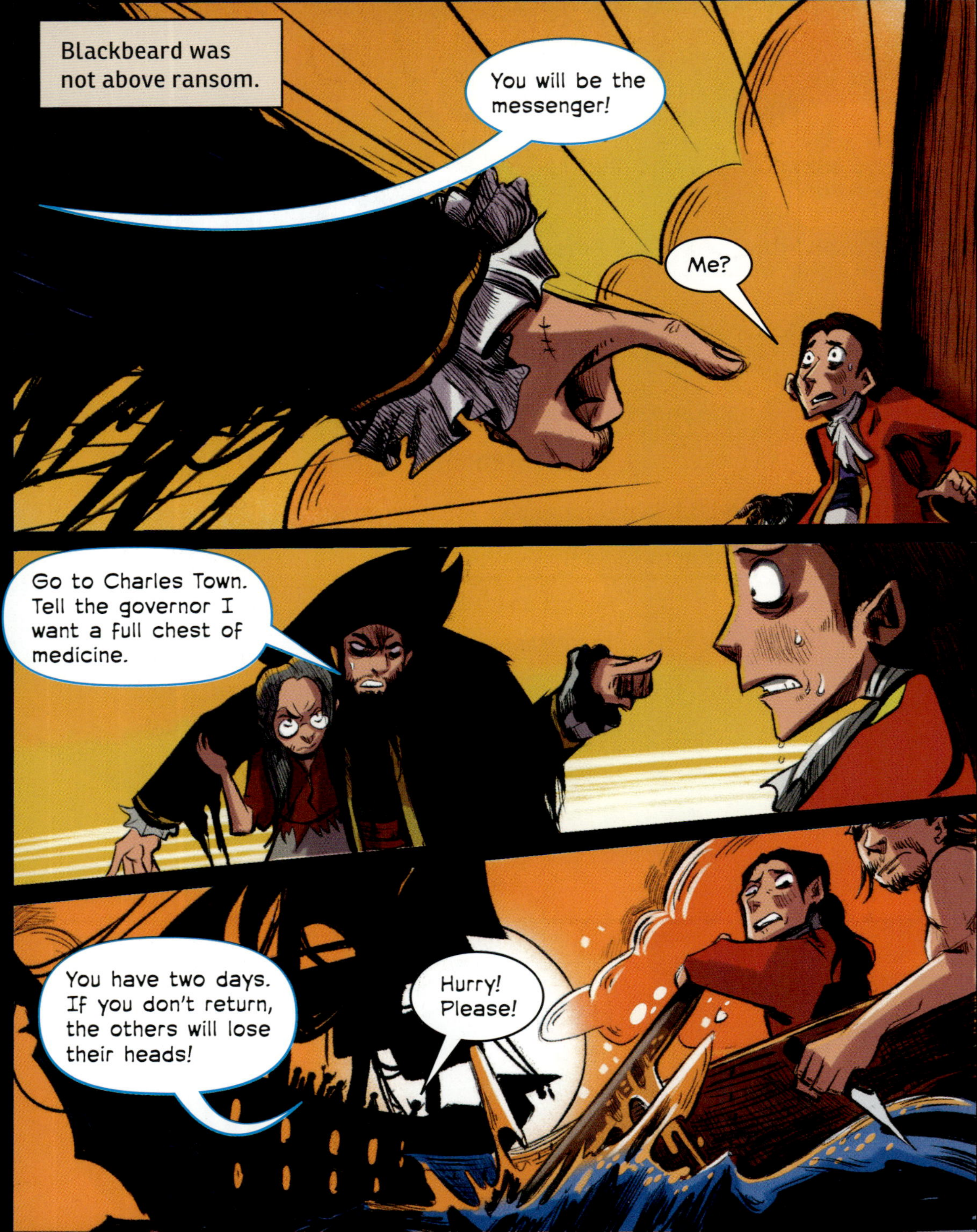
Blackbeard was not above ransom.
You will be the messenger!
Me?
Go to Charles Town. Tell the governor I want a full chest of medicine.
You have two days. If you don't return, the others will lose their heads!
Hurry! Please!

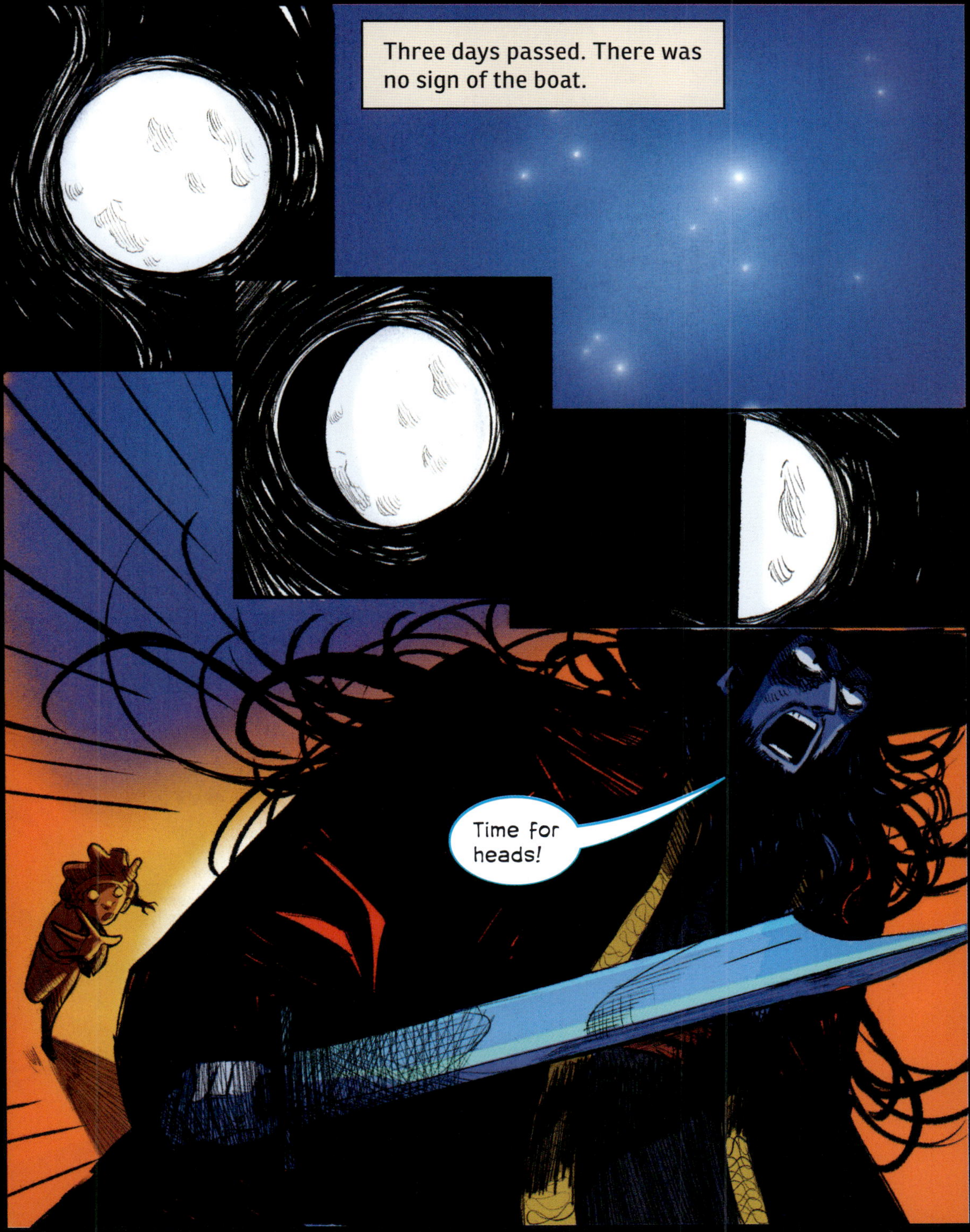
Three days passed. There was no sign of the boat.
Time for heads!

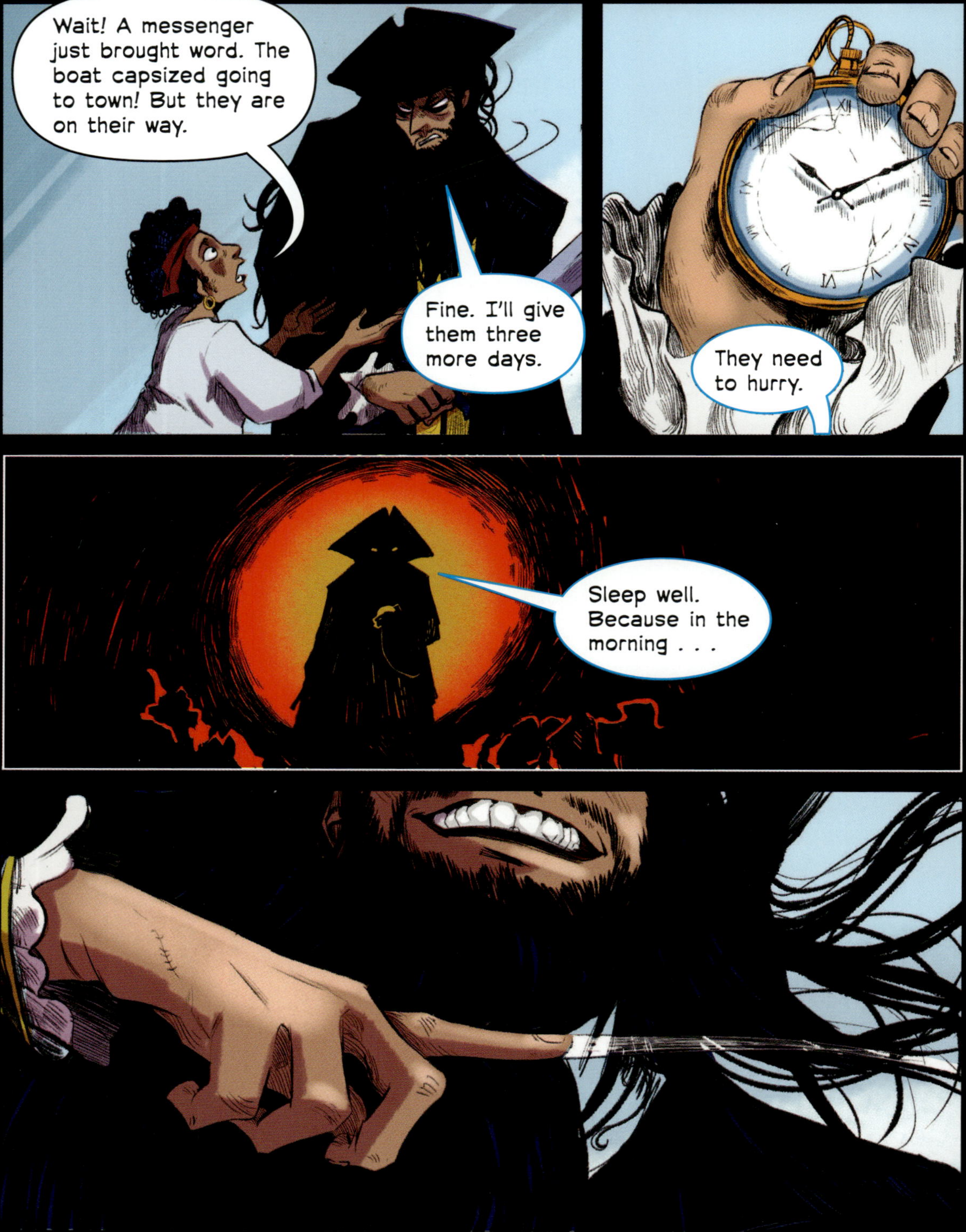
Wait! A messenger just brought word. The boat capsized going to town! But they are on their way.
Fine. I'll give them three more days.
They need to hurry.
Sleep well. Because in the morning . . .

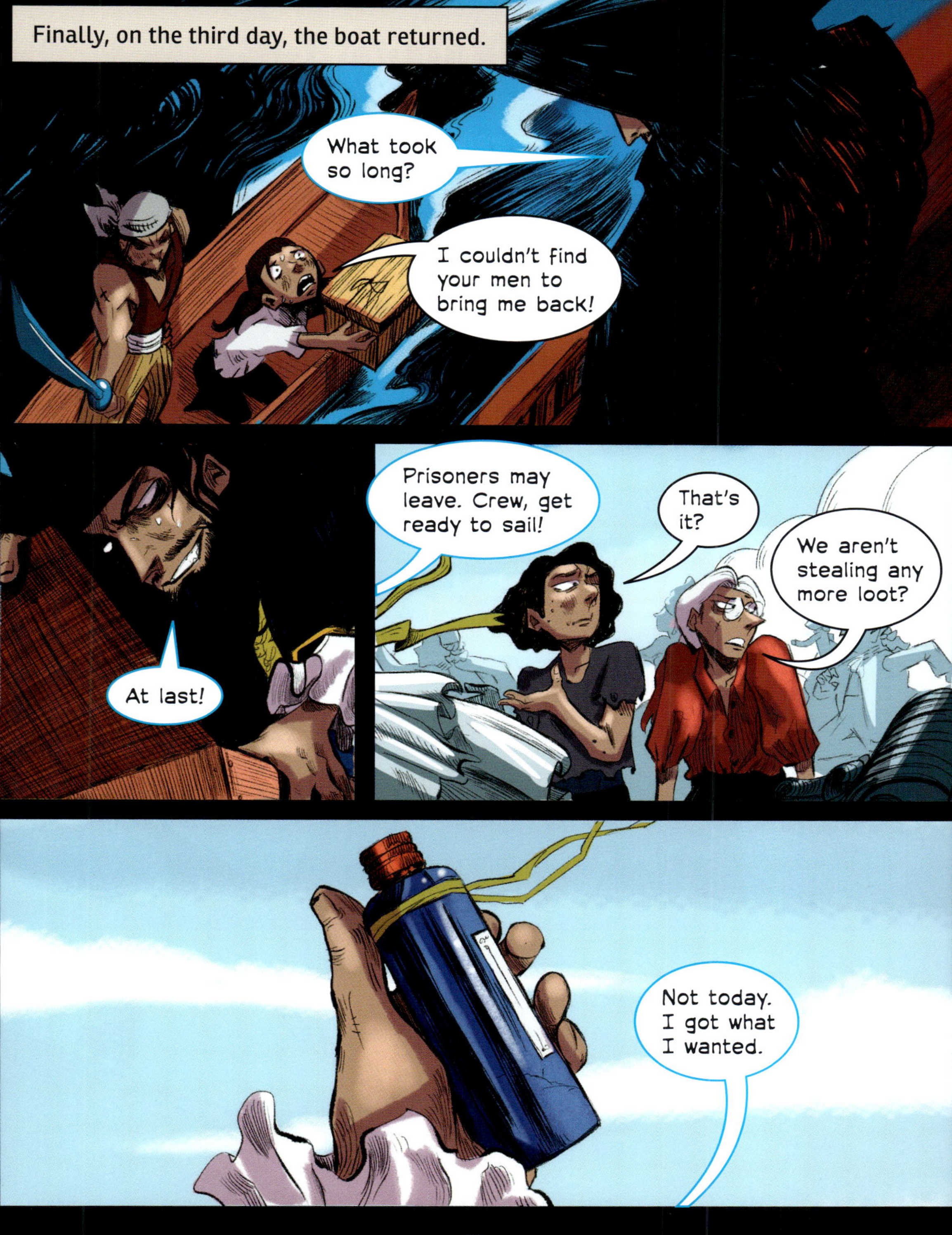
Finally, on the third day, the boat returned.
What took so long?
I couldn't find your men to bring me back!
At last!
Prisoners may leave. Crew, get ready to sail!
That's it?
We aren't stealing any more loot?
Not today. I got what I wanted.

CHAPTER 5

SAFE HARBORS

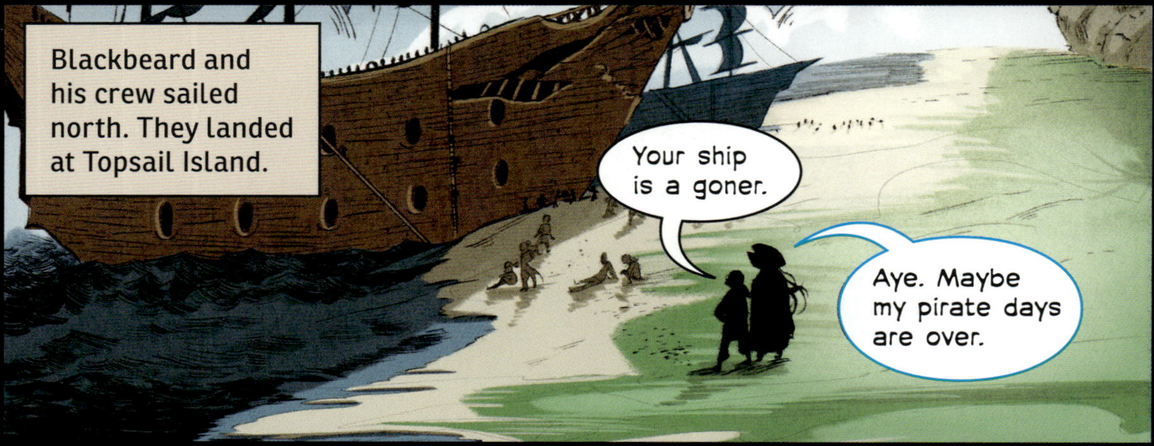
Blackbeard and his crew sailed north. They landed at Topsail Island.
Your ship is a goner.
Aye. Maybe my pirate days are over.

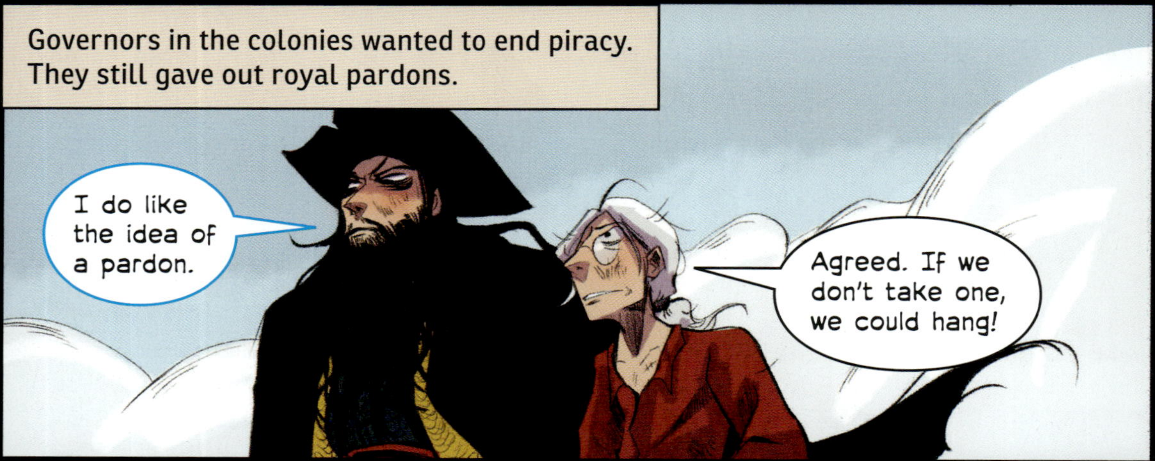
Governors in the colonies wanted to end piracy. They still gave out royal pardons.
I do like the idea of a pardon.
Agreed. If we don't take one, we could hang!

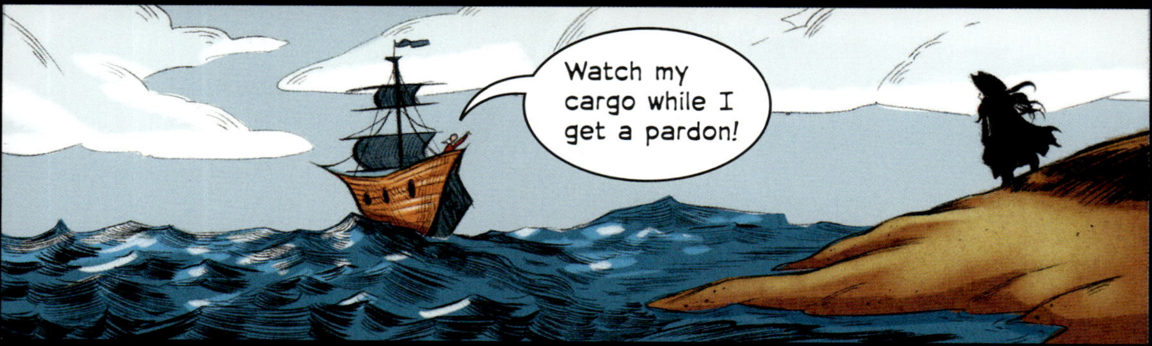
Watch my cargo while I get a pardon!

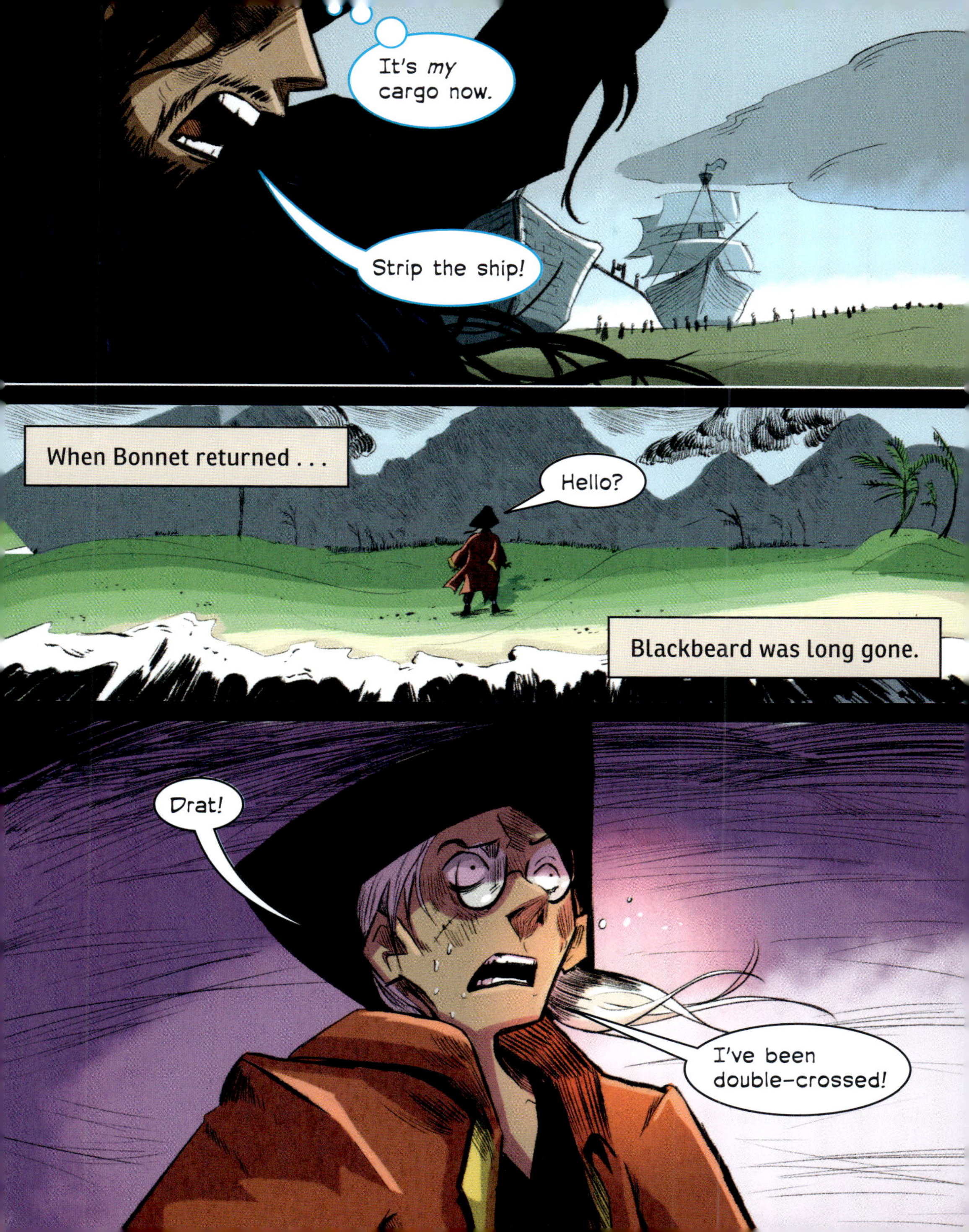

It's *my* cargo now.
Strip the ship!
When Bonnet returned . . .
Hello?
Blackbeard was long gone.
Drat!
I've been double-crossed!

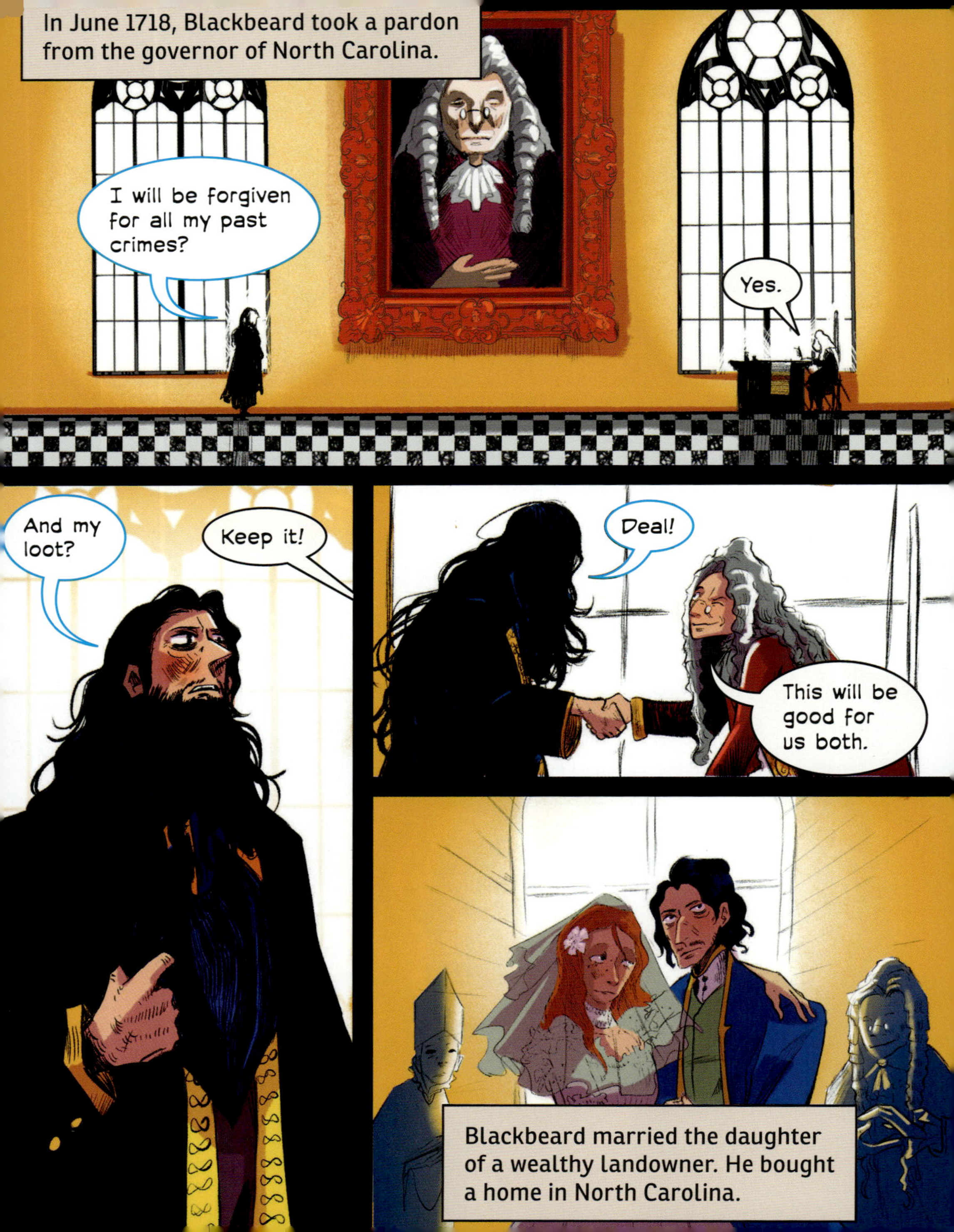
In June 1718, Blackbeard took a pardon from the governor of North Carolina.
I will be forgiven for all my past crimes?
Yes.
And my loot?
Keep it!
Deal!
This will be good for us both.
Blackbeard married the daughter of a wealthy landowner. He bought a home in North Carolina.

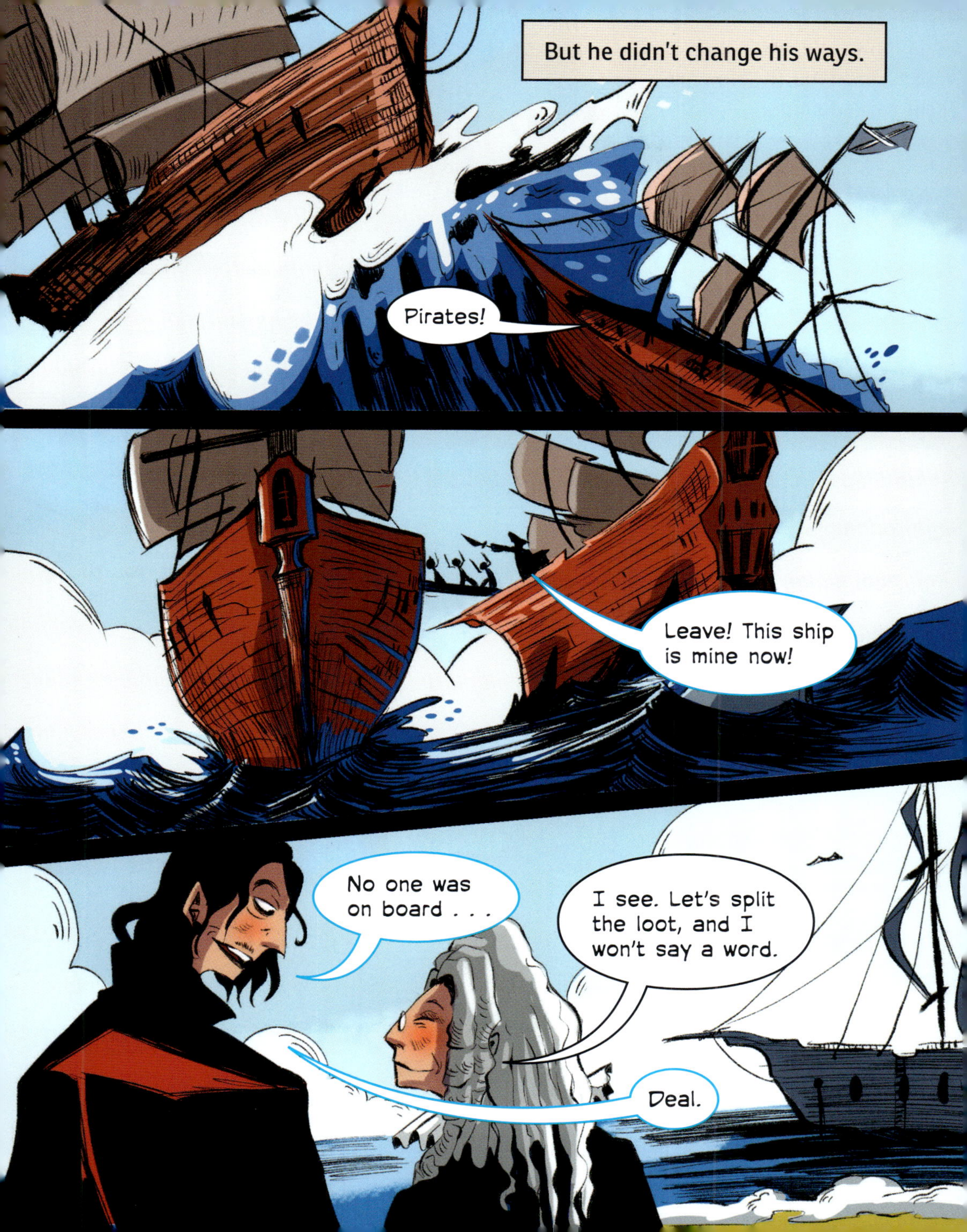
But he didn't change his ways.
Pirates!
Leave! This ship is mine now!
No one was on board . . .
I see. Let's split the loot, and I won't say a word.
Deal.

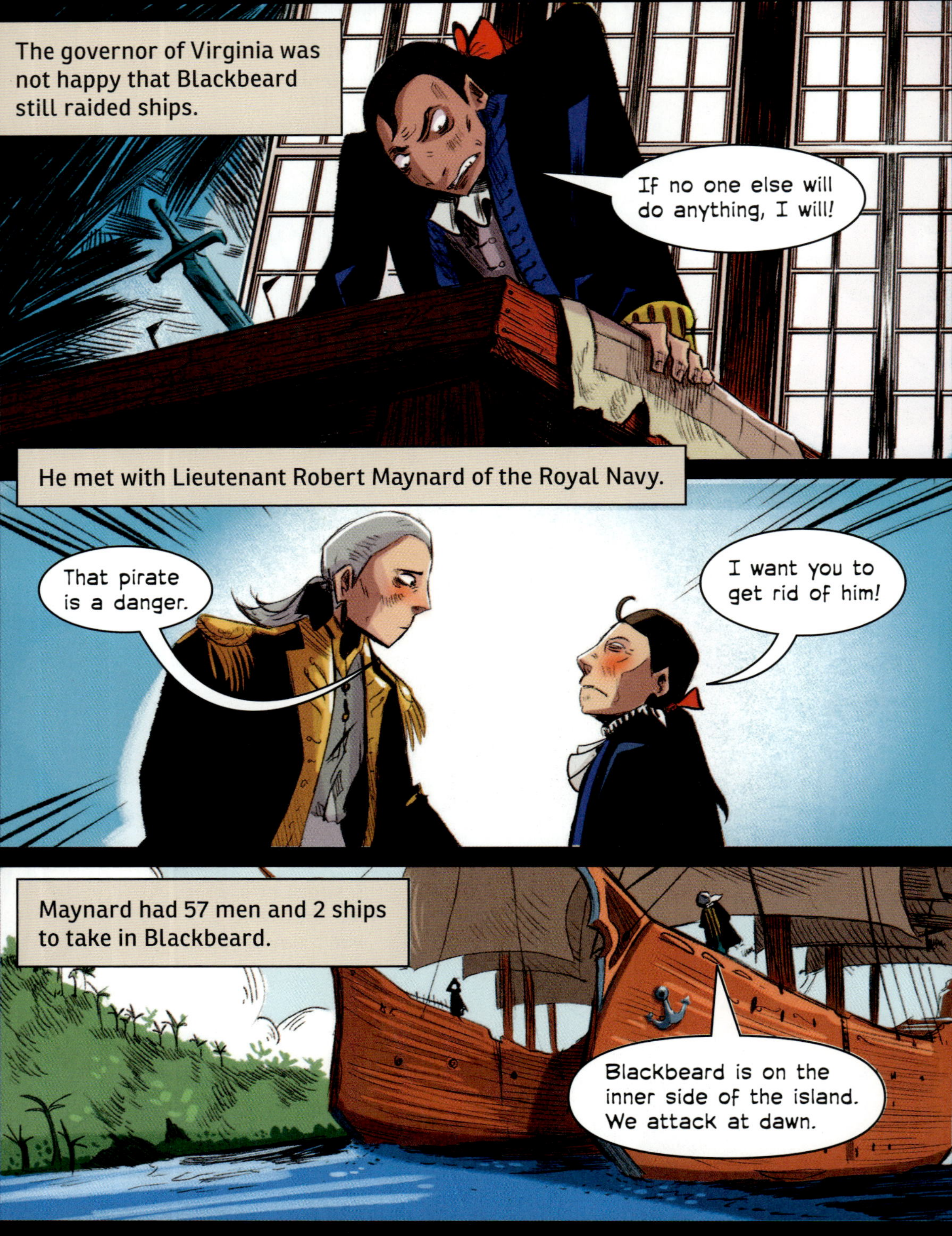
The governor of Virginia was not happy that Blackbeard still raided ships.
If no one else will do anything, I will!
He met with Lieutenant Robert Maynard of the Royal Navy.
That pirate is a danger.
I want you to get rid of him!
Maynard had 57 men and 2 ships to take in Blackbeard.
Blackbeard is on the inner side of the island. We attack at dawn.

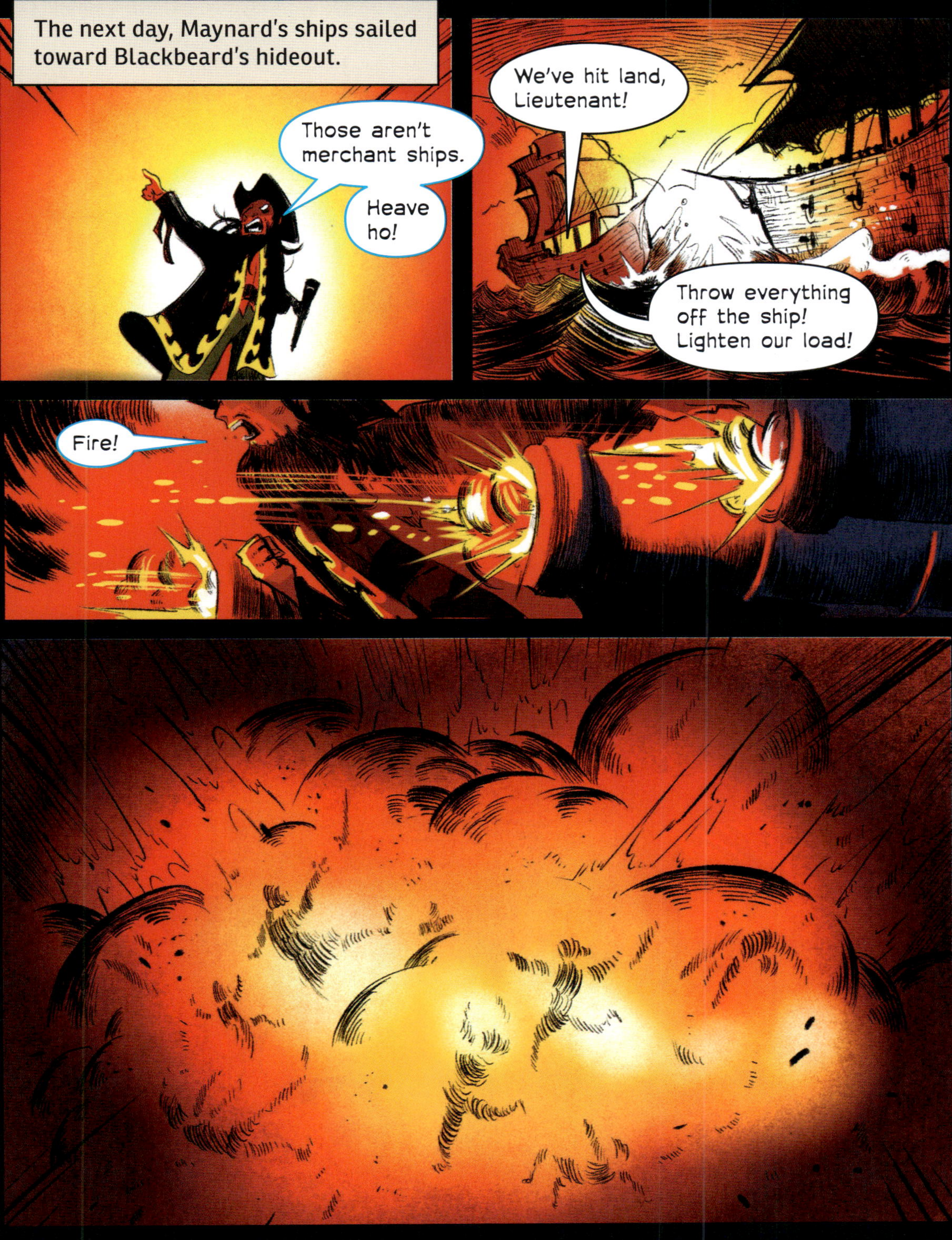
The next day, Maynard's ships sailed toward Blackbeard's hideout.
Those aren't merchant ships.
Heave ho!
We've hit land, Lieutenant!
Throw everything off the ship! Lighten our load!
Fire!

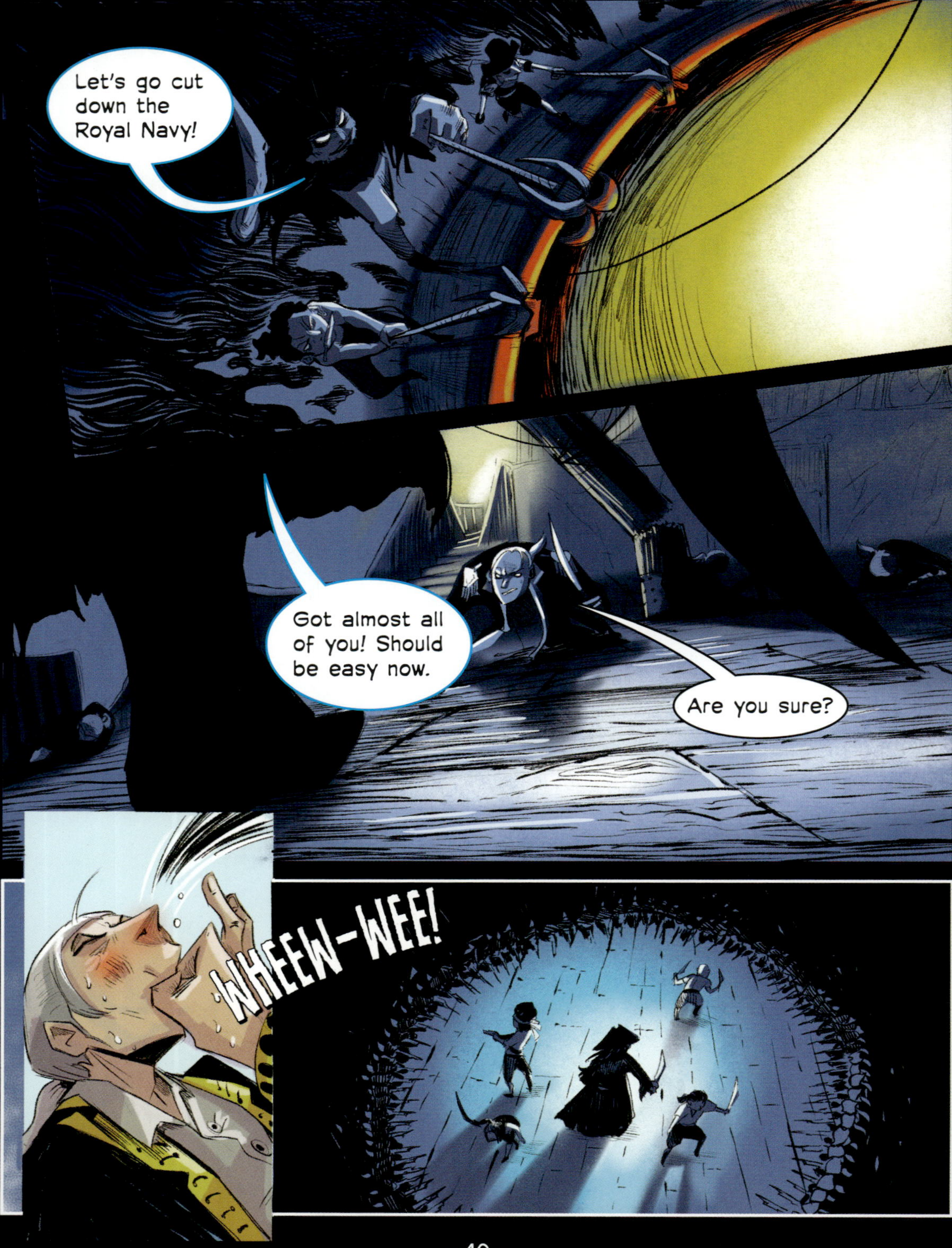
Let's go cut down the Royal Navy!
Got almost all of you! Should be easy now.
Are you sure?
WHEEW-WEE!

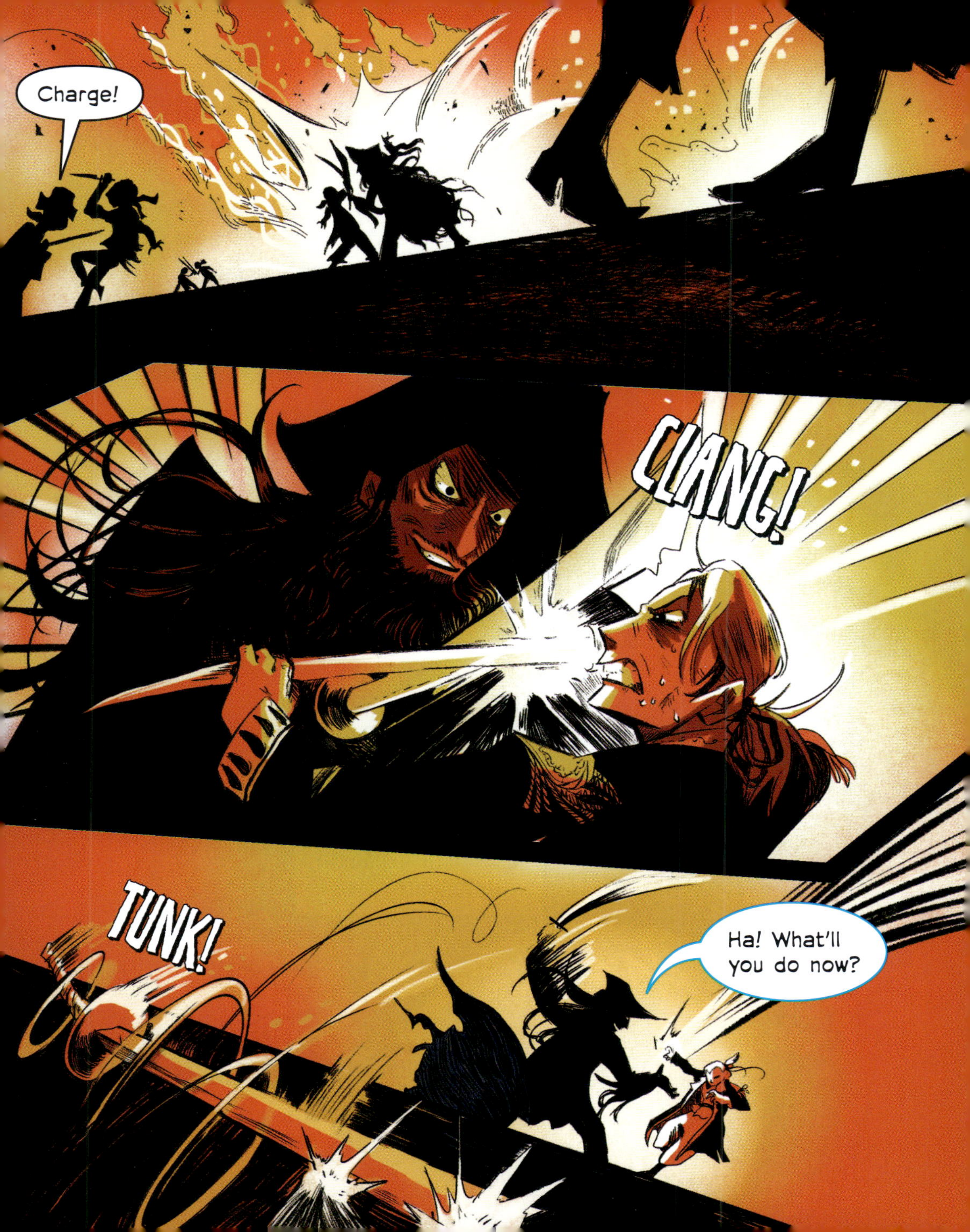
Charge!
CLANG!
TUNK!
Ha! What'll you do now?

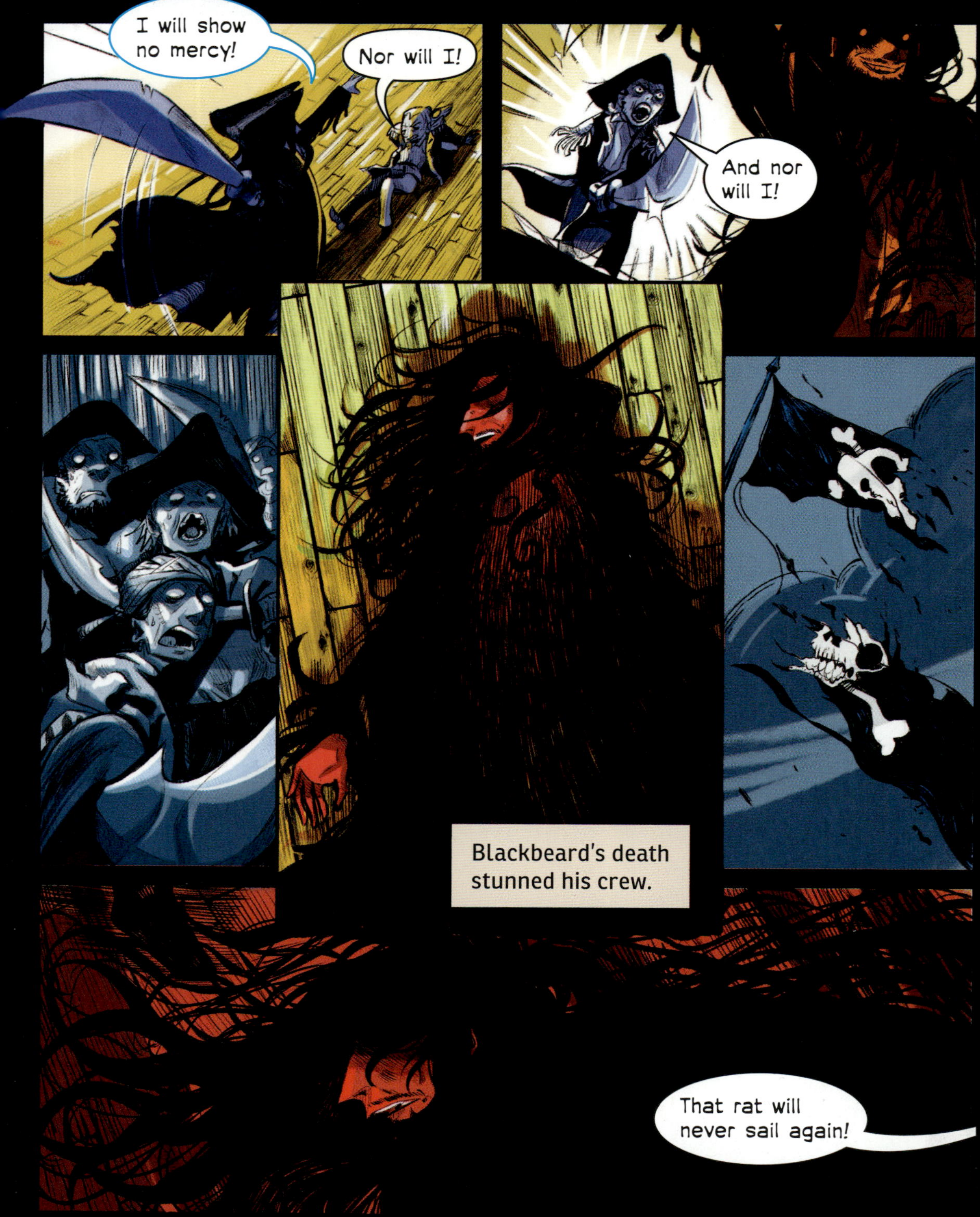
I will show no mercy!
Nor will I!
And nor will I!
Blackbeard's death stunned his crew.
That rat will never sail again!

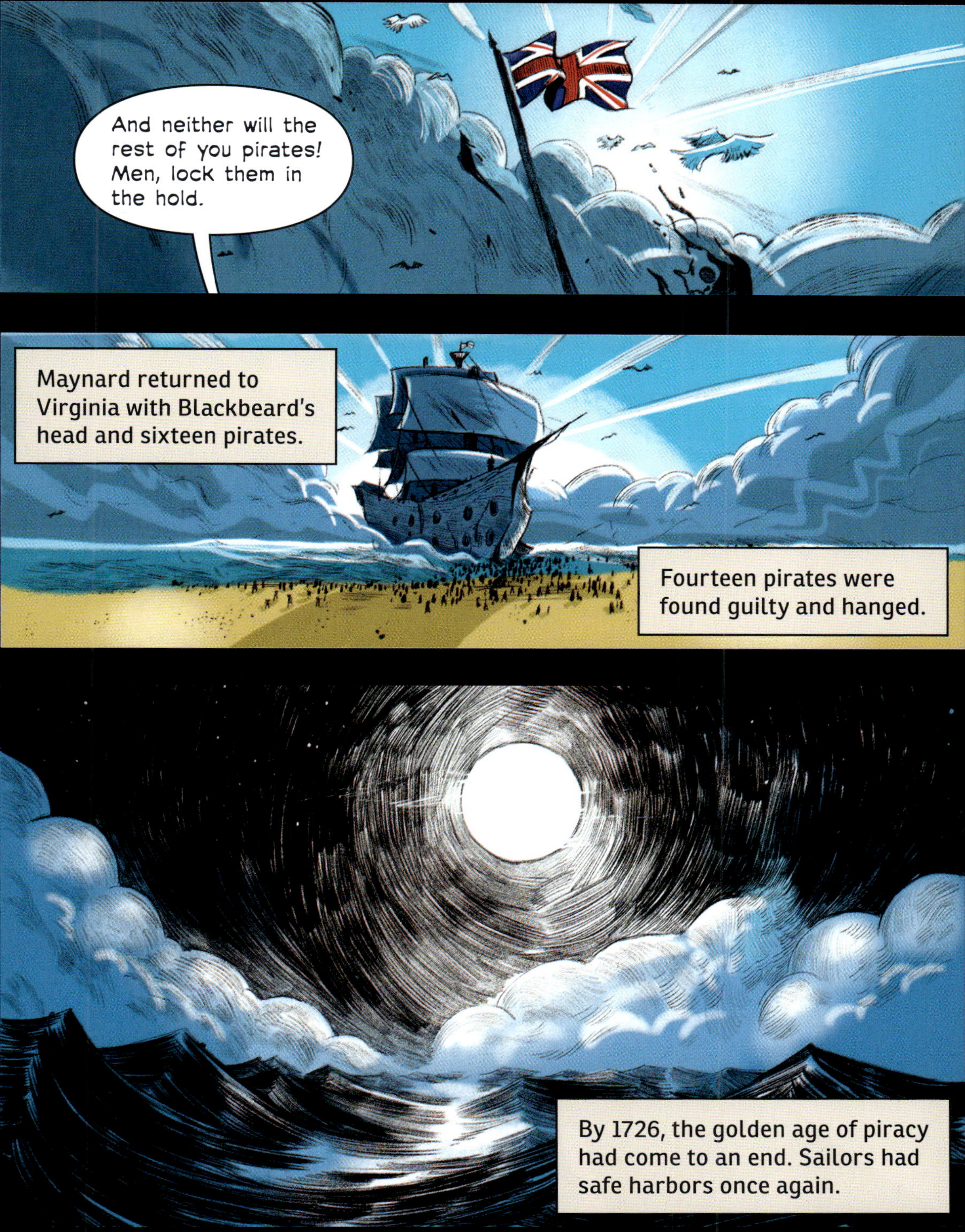
And neither will the rest of you pirates! Men, lock them in the hold.
Maynard returned to Virginia with Blackbeard's head and sixteen pirates.
Fourteen pirates were found guilty and hanged.
By 1726, the golden age of piracy had come to an end. Sailors had safe harbors once again.

MORE ABOUT BLACKBEARD

- Blackbeard was fierce. But there are no records that prove he killed anyone until his final battle with the Royal Navy.

- Blackbeard's first mate was named Israel Hands. Author Robert Louis Stevenson named a character after him in his 1883 novel, *Treasure Island*.

- Blackbeard's real last name is spelled many ways in records from his time. Some spellings include Teach, Tatch, Thach, and Tack.

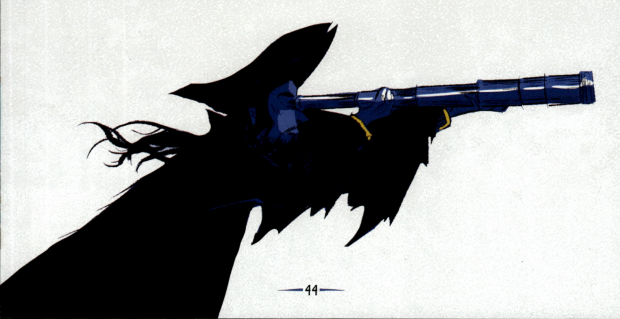

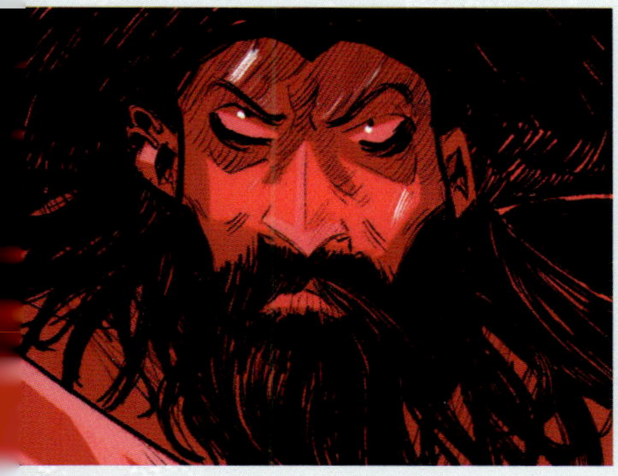

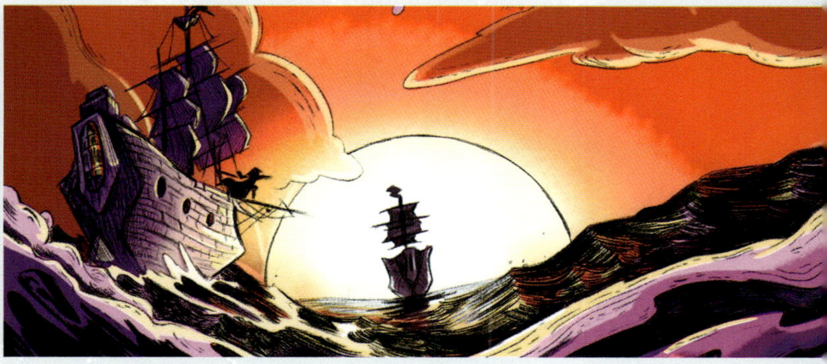

- Blackbeard may be one of the most well-known pirates, but others were more successful. Henry Avery took a ship worth hundreds of thousands of dollars. Black Bart Roberts seized hundreds of ships during his pirate career. Ching Shih was the most successful female pirate in history. She commanded more than 40,000 pirates.

- Blackbeard died in 1718. Nearly 300 years later, in 1996, divers found the sunken *Queen Anne's Revenge.* It was off the coast of North Carolina. The wreck included loaded cannons, an anchor, a diamond-studded glass, a sword, and a page from an adventure novel.

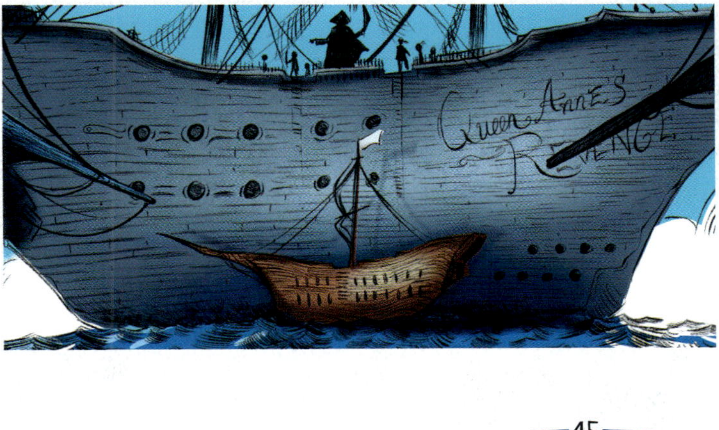
Queen ANNE'S REVENGE

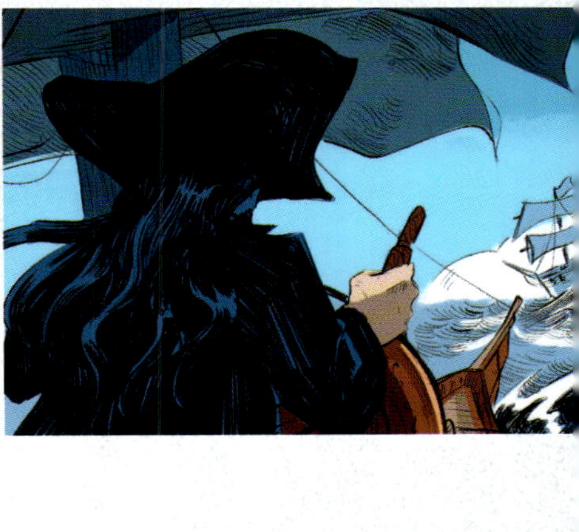

GLOSSARY

blockade (blok-AYD)—a closing off of an area to keep people or supplies from going in or out

capsize (KAP-syz)—to tip over in the water

governor (GUV-er-ner)—a person chosen to rule a specific area of land

letter of marque (LET-er UHV MARK)—a legal document allowing a ship's captain to claim the cargoes of enemy ships

loot (LOOT)—things that have been stolen or taken by force

merchant (MUR-chuhnt)—relating to or used in the buying and selling of goods for profit

pardon (PAHR-duhn)—an act of official forgiveness for a serious offense

plunder (PLUHN-der)—to steal things through force, often during battle

privateer (pry-vuh-TEER)—a ship licensed to attack and take goods from other ships; also, a sailor on such a ship

raid (RAYD)—a sudden attack on a place

ransom (RAN-suhm)—money or objects that are demanded before someone who is being held captive can be set free

surrender (suh-REN-der)—to give up and stop fighting

OTHER BOOKS IN THIS SERIES

NOTORIOUS PIRATES GRAPHICS
BLACK BART
DARING PIRATE OF THE ATLANTIC

NOTORIOUS PIRATES GRAPHICS
CHING SHIH
FAMOUS PIRATE COMMANDER

NOTORIOUS PIRATES GRAPHICS
GRACE O'MALLEY
PIRATE QUEEN OF IRELAND

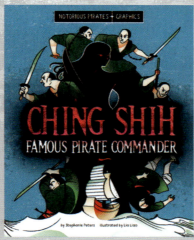

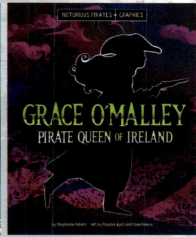

INTERNET SITES

Britannica Kids: Blackbeard
kids.britannica.com/students/article/Blackbeard/631920

Kiddle: Blackbeard Facts for Kids
kids.kiddle.co/Blackbeard

Southwestern University: A Treasury of Pirate Facts
southwestern.edu/live/news/14973-a-treasury-of-pirate-facts

ABOUT THE CREATORS

JESSICA GUNDERSON grew up in the small town of Washburn, North Dakota. She has a bachelor's degree from the University of North Dakota and an MFA in creative writing from Minnesota State University, Mankato. She has written more than 100 books for young readers. Her book *President Lincoln's Killer and the America He Left Behind* won a 2018 Eureka! Nonfiction Children's Book Silver Award. She currently lives in Madison, Wisconsin.

ANDI ESPINOSA is a freelance illustrator from the heat-infested realm of Miami, Florida. Eternally inspired by quirky characters and pencil textures, they are often on a quest to merge light, silliness, and wonder into dark, spindly, bug-eyed works. They currently illustrate children's books and book covers—and survive off tacos.

JOSE RAMOS is an acclaimed, versatile illustrator specializing in creating art for children. A featured artist at the global illustration agency IlloZoo, his work has appeared in numerous publications. His clients include Houghton Mifflin Harcourt, McGraw-Hill, and more.